REBIRTH OF WONDER

Mary Burritt
Christiansen
Poetry Series

Mary Burritt Christiansen Poetry Series

V. B. PRICE, SERIES EDITOR

Also available in the University of New Mexico Press
Mary Burritt Christiansen Poetry Series

Poets of the Non-Existent City,
    edited by Estelle Gershgoren Novak

Selected Poems of Gabriela Mistral,
    edited by Ursula K. Le Guin

Deeply Dug In,
    by R. L. Barth

Amulet Songs: Poems Selected and New,
    by Lucile Adler

In Company: An Anthology of New Mexico Poets,
    edited by Lee Bartlett, V. B. Price, and
    Dianne Edenfield Edwards

Tiempos Lejanos,
    by Nasario García

Refuge of Whirling Light: Poems,
    by Mary Beath

The River Is Wide/ El Río es Ancho:
    Twenty Mexican Poets, a Bilingual Anthology,
    edited and translated by Marlon L. Fick

A Scar Upon Our Voice,
    by Robin Coffee

CrashBoomLove: A Novel in Verse,
    by Juan Felipe Herrera

In a Dybbuk's Raincoat: Collected Poems,
    by Bert Meyers

Rebirth of Wonder

POEMS OF THE COMMON LIFE

David M. Johnson

Foreword by V. B. Price

Mark & Celina —
this is so fine that
our friendship grows
and prospers. Good luck
with your new future.
Dave [signature] 8-29-07

University of New Mexico Press ≣ Albuquerque

LIBRARY OF CONGRESS CATALOGING-IN-PUBLICATION DATA

Johnson, David M., 1939–
  Rebirth of wonder : poems of the common life /
David M. Johnson ; foreword by V.B. Price.
    p. cm. — (Mary Burritt Christiansen poetry series)
      ISBN-13: 978-0-8263-3975-1 (ALK. PAPER)
    I. Title.
    PS3610.O3345R43 2007
    811'.6—dc22

                    2006031821

Drawings by Karl Jacobson

Book and jacket design and type composition
    by Kathleen Sparkes

This book was typeset using Adobe Garamond
    and ITC Garamond Condensed

For Mona, wife and soulmate
     the many miles and all the adventures—
and children Peter, Sarah, and Maia
     their partners Roberta, Jeff, and Pete
For the energy and joy of grandchildren—
     Zola and David
For brother Arthur and the memory of father and mother.

At night in this waterless air [of the desert] the stars come down just out of reach of your fingers. In such a place lived the hermits of the early church piercing to infinity with unlittered minds. The great concepts of oneness and of majestic order seem always to be born in the desert. The quiet counting of the stars, and observation of their movements, came first from desert places.

—John Steinbeck

As soon as [the old gringo] entered Mexico his senses
had been awakened. Crossing the mountains and the desert,
he felt that he could hear and smell and taste and see as never
before, as if he were young again, better than young again—
he smiled—when lack of experience had prevented comparisons...
Here, now, amid the copper-colored mountains and the
shimmering, translucent evening and the odors of tortillas
and chiles, and the distant guitars...he could listen and
taste and smell almost supernaturally.

—Carlos Fuentes

It would be lovely if the places you visited opened you up,
made you more aware, startled you and made you reflect on
how much you loved your home place.

—Barry Lopez

Life without poetry would, I believe, be very much less worth living. I speak of poetry now as a natural human activity and state of awareness . . . It belongs to the world of hunger and sex— a kind of thought, but thought felt as bodily need and energy. Poetry is filled with memories of the physical impact of feelings and sensations, including especially the impact of sound and most especially of the human voice.

—M. L. Rosenthal

What is all this juice and all this joy?
    A strain of the earth's sweet being in the beginning
In Eden garden—

—Gerard Manley Hopkins

Contents

Foreword   xiii
Acknowledgments   xvii
Introduction   xix

I. Immigrants   1

Midwest   2
Third Generation   4
Patriarch in the Midwest   6
Dakota Territory   7
Birthright   8
Protestant Ethic   13
Migrations   14
Brotherly Advice in the 1950s   15
A Time of Amateurs   16
Changing Times   18
Mother at Ninety   19
Handkerchief   21
Night Song   22

II. First Taste of Mexico   23

The Gift   25
One-Wheel Trailer   27
Sopa   28
Tourist   29
Bilingual Means Having Two Tongues   30
Processional   31
Tlaquepaque   32
Marias   33
El Dia del Muerto   34

A Machete for Thorn and Prickly Pear   36
Face to Face   37
Day before Christmas   38
Jesús (Jesse) Chavez and Neighbors   40
Nuevo Laredo   42
This Is a Cup   43
One Afternoon in Tlaquepaque   44

III. Borderlands   47

Albuquerque's Mt. Calvary Cemetery   48
Jemez Mountains   49
Door-to-Door Chile   50
February in New Mexico   51
First Love   52
The City Limits   53
Collecting: A Modern Paradigm   54
Sarah's Songs   56
Grandfather Tree   57
Winter in Atlantic City 1970   59
Sitting on the World   61
Healing   62
State Fair   63
Connection   68
Father and Daughter Backpacking   69
Requiem on the Oregon Coast   70
Rain in Albuquerque   71
End of Autumn   72
Roots   74
Winter   75
Anniversary   77

IV. On the Road   79

    Winter on the Mediterranean   80

    Women in a Spanish Fishing Village   81

    Spanish Photograph   82

    Sex in Scotland   83

    Gino's in Stonehaven   84

    Reverie in Sweden   85

    The Almond in Winter   86

    Ancient Deities   87

    Innocence   88

    Eros   89

    The Greek Legacy   90

    Arkadi Monastery   92

    Leaving Crete   94

    Topless on Santorini   95

    The Gift of Language   96

    Lourdes of the Aegean   97

    Drum Majors in Istanbul   98

    Hagia Sophia   99

V. Mexico Magic   101

    Crossing Borders   102

    Mexican Pharmacy   105

    Salt Water   106

    North and South   108

    Markets   109

    Old and New   110

    Second-Class Bus   111

Isla de Janitzio   112

Spring Break in Mazatlán   114

Paradise   115

Roadkill   116

Maps   118

Mazatlán Airport   119

Timing is Everything   120

The Dust of Mexico   121

VI. The Common Life   123

Labyrinth   124

En Route to School in the East   125

Daughter of Eve   126

How Would You Like It, Dad?   127

Mastectomy   128

Take, for Example, Ralph   130

Neighbors Is Neighbors   132

After a Storm on the Costa del Sol   133

Millennium Two Thousand   134

Wondering about Things   136

Letter to Maia on Her Birthday   137

Bird Watching   140

Spring Rites   142

A Season without God   143

Epiphany   144

Emergence   145

Foreword

When a poet and mythographer as gifted as David Johnson looks at the "common life" in the prime of his journey as a writer, a rebirth of recognition and excitement is the gift he offers to his readers. Take the lines from a poem about Johnson's Norwegian heritage called "Birthright": "A boy's first breath in winter./Outside is a giant with frost on his teeth/so cold the trees crack open like thunder." Johnson knows how to focus the synergy of feeling and insight into powerful subliminal images that give awareness a rush of connection familiar in myth.

The poems in *Rebirth of Wonder: Poems of the Common Life* are the work of a master of this craft. Both short- and long-line prose poems chronicle Johnson's migrations and adventures of discovery from Minnesota to New Mexico, Mexico, Spain, and Greece, an odyssey that took him from a childhood as the son of a Lutheran minister to the life of a poet-teacher making his way in the world as a father, husband, grandfather, and man of tolerance and conscience in the wilds of the twentieth century.

In embracing and praising the "common life," Johnson's story-telling poems take the reader into the true worlds of people's lives, his own and his family's included, with images so clear you can feel them in your body. When he writes about his mother in "Birthright," he gives form to generations of consciousness, embodied in his mother's focus on serving the right and the good.

Mother loved a good blizzard
   a fresh blanket covering town and field
      the world swept pristine and new.

It was what she meant by righteousness.
   Not the cleansing of the heart, or the hand
      forgiven, but the refinement of will.

In winter it becomes perfectly clear
    like a black line across a white canvas.
        How then to preserve this certainty.

Polished windows and curtains, family linens
    pinned to the line. And clean, clean where no
        visitor went, obscure in attic or basement.

Dirt was like sin—a lack of discipline,
    a form of weakness.

Clean, direct, mysterious, and rich with understatement, Johnson's poems come from a person who knows how to pay attention to his life and to honor the lives of others. His poems have the same strength and grace of line, the same perfection of joinery, as Shaker furniture. They withstand many readings, growing in depth. They inspire in the way that only words from a wise, good heart can.

    He writes in "Roots" of a spiritual adventure through the drama of genetic recognition with one of his daughters in New Mexico:

Sarah and I climb the thirsty mesa, find a deep pocket
    for a fire. Ghosts made of mesquite blow over our heads.

I lift an old nest of wire and twig to the wind.
    It sings and hums a higher spell than the power lines.

We search for some silent pageant. Pieces of rabbit fur
    are clotted with cat tracks and blood.

We must learn to read these relics—fossilized antler, uncle's
    pocket watch, old oval photographs in the steamer truck.

Ancestors are tiny bones that catch in the throat. Strange
    tongues—trolls and gnomes hide in the closet.

We are immigrants, the lost and found of every generation.
    Our roots grow lengthwise.

No wonder Johnson's teaching of creative writing over the last thirty
years or so has been one of the reasons why New Mexico is filled
with so many poets and writers of such extraordinary quality. A
mythographer, editor, classics scholar, author, and widely antholo-
gized poet, Johnson has written works that include the introduction
to ancient Greek and Roman literature in *The Bedford Anthology of
World Literature*, which he coedited, and the classics introduction in
Western Literature in a World Context by St. Martin's Press, which he
also coedited. His writing on mythology has appeared in *Parabola*
where he did a major translation of Nahuatl mythology. He is the
author of *Word Weaving: A Creative Approach to Teaching and
Writing Poetry*, published by The National Council of Teachers, as
well as the coeditor of *Talking from the Heart: An Anthology of Men's
Poetry*, among many other publications.

    Rebirth of Wonder alerts readers on every page to the possibility
of waking up to an enlivened recognition of the wonders of the
inner realities of their own daily lives. You can't ask more than that
from a book of poems.

                                    V. B. Price
                                    Albuquerque, June 2006

Acknowledgments

Some of these poems appeared in the following magazines and journals: *Crosswinds, Century: A Southwest Journal of Observation and Opinion, Conceptions Southwest, Rio Grande Writers Quarterly, Man, Alive! A Journal of Men's Wellness, Writers Forum, The Christian Century, The New Mexico Independent, Puerto del Sol, Southwest Heritage, New Laurel Review, The New Mexico Humanities Review, Shepherd's Pie, Out of Sight, Café Solo, Wind, New Mexico Magazine, Albiero Quarterly, New America: A Review, The Margarine Maypole Orangoutang Express, Loco Motives, Au Verso, New Mexico Quarterly, Blackberry, Ironwood;* and in the anthologies *Voices from the Rio Grande* (A Rio Grande Writers Association Press Book, 1976), *The Indian Rio Grande: Recent Poems from 3 Cultures* (San Marcos Press, 1977), *Southwest: A Contemporary Anthology* (Red Earth Press, 1977), *Unexpected Events: Poems from Writers in New Mexico* (The Hawk Press, 1984), *Talking from the Heart* (Men's Network Press, 1990), *The Spirit that Wants Me: A New Mexico Anthology* (Duff, Inc., 1991), *In Company: An Anthology of New Mexico Poets after 1960* (University of New Mexico Press, 2004). Some of these poems were also published in chapbooks: *Pilgrim Country* (San Marcos Press, 1976), *The Oldest Song* (San Marcos Press, 1983), *Altar to an Unknown God* (Solo Press, 1990), *Fire in the Fields* (Writers on the Plains, 1996). Grateful acknowledgment is made to the editors and publishers.

A special thanks to Glenna, Cort, Dave, Barrett, Barry, Victor, Pat and Rudy, Pat Smith, Jake, David, and to my mentor, Gene Frumkin, for encouragement. And to the memory of E. W. Tedlock.

Introduction

Events in the United States during the 1960s—the assassinations and the Vietnam War, the marches for civil rights and attendant violence—shaped my generation. To some of us it seemed as if a divided and divisive America had lost its way. Shattered was the possibility of beliefs that might have provided coherence and vision for the second half of the twentieth century.

It became the role of contemporary poetry, as well as the other arts, to once again explore the lens through which reality is viewed and to examine the basic ingredients out of which a meaningful picture of the world might be constructed: the hidden self, the dynamics of family and friendship, the tension between secular and sacred, peace and justice—all against the backdrop of history and tradition. With multiple voices and perspectives, this process of attending to and healing a conflicted world of wars and disasters continues to the present day.

I was born into the Midwestern world of Norwegian-Lutheran ministers: father and grandfather, brother and cousins. Young men of a similar background to mine talked about the ministry like sons of ranching families in Montana might talk about a life with horses and cows—why not? While I was in high school and college, family friends would regularly ask me, What year in seminary are you? After all, there was a direct pipeline from St. Olaf College to Luther Seminary in St. Paul, Minnesota. Honor is due to the founding fathers and mothers who settled the upper Midwest, their courage and sacrifice, their devotion to books and baccalaureate, but children of immigrants often continued the journey in the New World by moving on beyond their birthplace. My personal experiences in the pew on Sunday mornings and in religion classes during the week did not open up the mysterious dimension of the spirit or the life of the imagination, but served rather to cover them over with theological speculation and the trappings of social piety. Nevertheless this history was a sufficient prod to leave home.

After miles of travel, I discovered that epiphanies resulted from crossing some kind of boundary, leaving behind the telephone and my usual identity. I learned something about the sacred when Michael Tzakakis and I were a visiting a small chapel on the island of Crete. He said that the reason for filling a votary lamp from a barrel, setting a wick, and lighting it, was to get olive oil all over your hands—the infusion of the sacramental with the ordinary and material. I have always been better at looking in the distance than seeing things up close. I like horizons and remote mountains. On beaches I stare at the muffled strip where water meets sky, the big patterns where centuries melt into millennia. Writing poems, however, brings a closeness to my experience.

The act of writing slows down the bustle in the head, and brings an awareness of the present, right at the tip of the pen—not knowing what is going to be written, to be open to possibility, to each turn of letter, each turn of punctuation. Being right there as the world is born, like a bud unfolding. Not rushing it, but slowing down, drifting into the process of birth. Not to race ahead of the pen to conclusions and fine phrases, but to stay close, to bear down with each stroke of the pen, touching the paper, feeling very much that the bare paper has a role in the process, that letters become words by shaping the emptiness of the page. A stick pokes the earth, a stick draws figures in the dust, the figures open their mouths and speak.

Then, given that attention, I open to another direction, another part of consciousness, paying attention to what's going on beyond the page: the rise and fall of sounds, the growing chorus of music in the pines—not cold, but just cool enough to remind me of winter, as if winter is out there somewhere waiting—or slowly advancing, sending out news of his arrival, words caught up in the wind playing among the needles. The laughter of children racing up the street on their bikes.

In a tribal parable of the Winnebago people, a wise grandfather describes the journey of life to his grandson as a series of passages that one needs to cross over or pass through: deep ravines, a woods filled with thorns and weeds, threatening birds, a great fire encircling the earth, dense forests, and perpendicular bluffs. Whether these obstacles represent anger, suffering, or death, the grandfather assures his listener that the teachings of the lodge and the footprints of medicine men provide a map for meeting life's challenges. Road signs have a similar function, as do poems.

In both Greece and Mexico, highways are marked with crosses or roadside shrines where individuals have died in traffic accidents— a tangible mark of someone's passing. It is appropriate to also mark a life-giving experience with a poem or piece of prose, where the commonplace, having been elevated in its uniqueness, is celebrated.

The poems in this collection comprise a series of guideposts from my journey, an imaginative compass for charting the familiar, as well as those patches of geography that remain obscure and ambiguous. Signs are useful for marking dangerous curves, warnings about detours and dead ends, as well as side roads to vistas and human drama. Those places where life changes direction. If all goes well, there is a kind of alternating rhythm between shadow and epiphany: days, when you question why you ever left home in the first place, when everything inside shakes loose, are followed by days of yellow flowers, kind words from neighbors, and pelicans dive-bombing in the bay.

In addition to pinning labels on the features of a passing landscape, a poem—at its best—leads us to identify with the young laborer slipping across the border. The aging, white-haired lady in the supermarket who fumbles for change and holds up the entire checkout line.

I ⚜ Immigrants

They came over. They packed their belongings, and leaving the old world and all that was familiar and homely, they set out for the new world. Hunger drove them, the gods and their neighbors drove them. They followed their dreams, they followed the footsteps of those few who always go ahead into the unknown.

Whether it took days, weeks, or years, whether they came by land or in the hold of some smelly ship, whether they settled on a farm or in a city, the journey would continue, from one generation to the next.

Some settled down, sank roots. Others, like the Vikings of old, moved on. Unsettled, searching. A few came to realize that "home" is not necessarily a place, that the journey itself had become, in its way, home.

Midwest

From the hills of the lake country the road opens
    to great sheets of land and sky
        laid simply end to end.

How easy now to move across these borders
    after grandfather took hold of his dreams, a handful
        squeezed from squat red farms in Norway.

The past was hunger, outstripping the hillsides.
    The old world thought the new was a black mouth
        eating their sons. Their sons afraid to look back.

Pioneers west in sod huts and homesteads.
    Behind the harvest, another history—long winter
        nights, blizzards that rattled the mind.

Then silence. So thick and lonely it filled the ears.

2

Progress raised the capital in St. Paul—a place for
    pilgrimage—children brought there in school buses,
        told how America was made in the heartland.

The evergreens were axed and John Deere cut his teeth
    on tractors. The smell of malt sweetened the air,
        the noise of industry was honest profit.

Farmers brought in real culture from the East Coast,
    bought tickets to the symphony and life insurance.
        Sat on school boards, drove Buicks around town.

In one generation, English replaced Norwegian
    in classroom and church. Ibsen and Ole Rölvaag
        became old-fashioned electives at St. Olaf College.

We were told that settlers and citizens followed pioneers.

Third Generation

1

The family looked like the farm.
    A patriarch carved the turkey, prayed in Norwegian
        locked the door at night.

A few mothers went to college, were shuttled
    into home ec, shorthand or nursing. Became teachers,
        and got married.

My mother's bright light, surrounded by sewing circles
    and Ladies Aid—she could have been President.
        Her regret and anger still ride my bones.

Fathers couldn't be both frontier and friend.
    Some fought the long winter of work and wages
        with a stiff collar and spine.

I knew men who never kissed the ones they loved most,
    faces fixed for the north. Their sons
        turning in every direction for the blessing.

Neighbors held a handful of earth the way city people
    prayed, calluses planted like corn in the hot sun.
        The unsung heroes of seedtime and the next generation.

2

We grew up knowing that any man wedded to history
    was old country and smorgasbord—yet in him
        our only wedge against failure in the future.

The past was over, be anything you want—
    any doctor or lawyer, any professor or president.
        The sky was no longer the limit.

Every tree and highway had been planted or cut.
    Be a preacher like your dad.
        One's fate measured by the myth of America.

But it didn't always work—like filling your son's pack
    with ancestral dreams, then asking him
        to walk into space, at the head of his class.

I had friends who weren't as tall as their fathers' flour mills,
    who stared into the face of failure, knowing the god
        of Martin Luther was distant, yet demanding.

3

We spent most of our youth moving from the Midwest.
    All the bars in New York saying benedictions to St. Paul,
        the old cycle of suffering and righteousness.

On the far side of a desert, in another part of the country,
    I put down new roots, raised a family.
        So much is forgiven from a distance.

Patriarch in the Midwest

Where grandfather dipped his pen I burn incense. His inkwell
    a bronze pagoda laced with oriental trees and fern.

Winged serpents crawl along the tray, a butterfly etched in the roof
    waits to rise with the smoke of sandalwood.

Grandfather was a dragon from the north whose nature rejected
    the mystical East, the solitary path to Nirvana.

Jehovah wasn't a breath from within, but a force like a winter storm.
    Sin could destroy the household or locusts reap the harvest.

Did Scandinavians travel too far inland losing sight of the sea?
    All that snow filling the hollows in a man's mind.

Grandfather talked to God in English and Norwegian, like engaging
    the captain of a ship. His sermons charted the open spaces,

As if words could finally cut clear between good and evil.
    From his pulpit in Minnesota Grandfather could see the ocean.

Dakota Territory

There are two eyes in the human head . . . The prairie eye looks
for distance, clarity, and light; the woods eye for closeness,
complexity, and darkness . . . The prairie is endless!

—Bill Holm

Years before I saw it
elevators jutted erect out of the grasslands—
amazed and awkward banners announcing
a stand of poplars, a few frame houses,
a dry goods store: threaded by iron rails,
a steam-driven artery moving to the horizon
beyond the tip of your finger
safe in bushels and a new spur.

Fargo grows like a wild weed on the prairie—
barbecues and patios past the city limits.
Sears sends credit cards with the catalogue,
suits and overalls walk side by side.
And West Fargo—home of the sixteenth
largest stockyard in the world.

Even so, downtown, at the very center,
a few of the old pillared homes are for sale.
An unsavory crowd frequents the bars near the tracks.
Some cities like giant ponderosa get heart rot in their prime.
Last December the run of the Great Northern Railway—
Fargo to St. Paul—was canceled, a possible omen.

Birthright

Brother would tease him, tell him he
    was an accident of Norway's long winters
        his folks huddled together in Oslo.

He came as father came, the northern lights
    lighting the way into mother
        her dark depths hidden from the sun.

A secret conception, like a tail disappearing—
    there was simply a womb, a salt sea
        a night journey.

He was a fish, a tongue with scales
    in a liquid labyrinth
        swimming towards the blood.

He was a bird, a flight of feathers
    a fledgling searching
        for a cleft in the sky.

2

A boy's first breath in winter.
    Outside is a giant with frost on his teeth
        so cold the trees crack open like thunder.

The chambers of Ymir's mind slowly fill
    with the silence of falling snow. Ravens
        nest in the empty socket of his right eye.

3

Mother loved a good blizzard
   a fresh blanket covering town and field
      the world swept pristine and new.

It was what she meant by righteousness.
   Not the cleansing of the heart, or the hand
      forgiven, but the refinement of will.

In winter it becomes perfectly clear
   like a black line across a white canvas.
      How then to preserve this certainty.

Polished windows and curtains, family linens
   pinned to the line. And clean, clean where no
      visitor went, obscure in attic or basement.

Dirt was like sin—a lack of discipline,
   a form of weakness.

4

Small Midwest town hankering for corn and cows.
   Saturday nights for shopping, and "How'er the crops?"
      Hamms beer washed the husks out of the throat.

Bars were saloons, a raucous, midnight music.
   Patrons on barstools turned away from the window
      when the preacher's kid walked past.

When dad was a kid, he'd take his father's pail
    to the local brewery, fill it up for him,
        then stop halfway home for a sample.

As a Lutheran minister dad modeled sobriety.
    "Isn't it too bad," he'd say, "that things in life
        that taste so good are bad for you?"

5

Mother always knew when he came home
    from the pool hall. Cigarette and beer smell,
        his fascination with the wizards of twilight.

Howard Stock with his magic cue, white shirt and overalls.
    Not much of a farmer, he pampered those stripes and
        solids like his own children, picking up some change.

And Donny Siebold, a ne'er-do-well in the workaday world,
    but an artist on green felt. His delicate hands danced
        around the snooker table, pocket to pocket.

After the homecoming pep rally, Don ran drunk down the street
    torching piles of leaves, his own fireworks and snake dance.
        A few more years and his liver gave out.

6

Father would say, we don't have the leaders now
we had back then, men of character and vision,
building the future with banks and churches,
filled to the rafters with corn and principles.

Something upright
settled the Midwest
to walk and work upright
unbending, uplifting
no backsliding or drifting.

Held tight to the plow
upright the white-sided house
the red barn, beacon for miles
standing upright like silos
and grain elevators.

Straight the backbone
stiff the spine
upright the preachers
upright fathers and families
pillars of the community.

Heroes of renunciation
and righteousness
the right hand of God
a proper piety
piercing the heavens.

No wonder they feared alcohol and sex, playing cards
and dancing—any lubricant for the soul. Early immigrants
sent to Norway for their clergy, to defy those ghosts
rising like sin from the frozen earth.

7

Yearly my cousin in Trondheim rents a small boat
    and rows into the North Sea. He survived the Nazis,
        the Russians, one swell after another.

My grandfather joins him holding hard to the rudder,
    then my father with his strong swimmer's hands
        and long steady strokes.

Mentors arrive to navigate the deep. I sit beside them,
    take one of the oars. We pull for the aurora borealis
        leaping and boiling across the sky.

Protestant Ethic

I cannot take credit for any of this, the schools and churches,
the ice cream parlors and the Sears mail-order store—the bustling
prosperity of middle-class Midwest. It was all in place when I was
born: the electricity and flush toilets, the tanks and airplanes.

Public schools trained the kids in civics and the work ethic,
the police kept order on Saturday nights, told our parents where
we parked with girls, whether we drank beer.

It has not changed much. Those of us born since the Great
Depression have simply added to the machinery, more chrome
and toasters. An old high school classmate now has her own
tennis court and swimming pool.

Migrations

Yearly the migrations, like chaff kicked up along the road.
    Set adrift by plague or pollution, a job in the next generation.

Almost before we leave home someone else moves in,
    lives in the old house, doesn't keep it up.

Spaniards left Spain years ago, Norwegians / Norway,
    New Yorkers / New York. The West slides into the sea.

No more natives anywhere / migrants who haven't learned
    the folk songs, the region's dances.

Children forget their parents and settle in the next city.
    Home is no longer a place, but the journey itself.

Having moved beyond all physical boundaries, we look
    backward to mark some sign of our passing.

A foreigner stares back in the mirror, memories fill with
    old keys, photo albums and the national anthem.

Brotherly Advice in the 1950s

Older brother sat on the other side of my bedroom. Mother had called him home from the seminary in St. Paul to talk to his teenage brother about sex. Father had dealt with the topic by solemnly giving his sons a book about the evils of masturbation. None of the participants seemed to appreciate the marvelous irony of the City's namesake and sexuality.

What d'ya been doing anyway? elder brother asked.

Some necking, I said, staying out late. You remember those high bluffs overlooking Lake St. Croix? At night the cars in the distance like pearl buttons on a blouse...

How old are you now? he cut in, getting impatient.

Not always there, I went on, but near those Indian mounds, that look like large breasts, those trees in the park that kinda moan when they rub together...

Stop it! he shouted, tossing some darkness towards the kitchen where mother awaited the results of her call for aid.

Don't tell me anymore! My god, I don't care.

Exiting the room, he growled, Do what you want, just keep your zipper zipped!

A Time of Amateurs

In line for the chairlift, a fellow saw my skis and said, I hope you don't mind, but they're antiques. I wish I had a pair to hang up. Are they really wood?

Hickory, I replied, a type of wood.

He said, My mother refinished her wood skis and hung them over the fireplace. How old are yours?

Over twenty years, I said, probably older than you. These have steel edges, but my first pair used strips of innertube to fasten my boots.

Father brought back wood skis from Norway in 1939 with leather bindings that buckled around the heel. The tips curled up like slippers worn by gnomes. His father made him skis from barrel staves. They always stuck at the bottom of the straw pile and he'd fly head over teakettle.

Dad first took me skiing on the hills behind Tostrud's farm. We sidestepped up the slope, packing the snow, then skied straight down. Climbed back up again and down. Sometimes we left our bamboo poles at the top, spread our arms and swooped like two blackbirds into the stubbled cornfield.

Walking back to the car past the cow barn and manure pens, he always asked, Smell that? Take a deep breath! In the car, he'd threaten to stop by some pungent farm to remind us, Don't forget your roots.

Dad had his best skiing in Norway visiting relatives. Trains left Oslo hourly, taking skiers into the mountains. The whole day was spent gliding and drifting back into town. Huts along the route provided warmth and food.

Trollhaugen was the first ski area in Wisconsin close-by. Rope tows and aching shoulders. If someone ahead fell in the track on the way up, you let the rope slip through your leather mitts, turning them black. You could burn through two or three pair in a season.

Music was piped out over the trails, songs like "Mockingbird Hill" and yodeling. We dreamed about going further north to higher hills and longer runs, Mt. Telemark or Lutsen on Lake Superior, but that meant motels and eating out.

Dad brought our fashions back from the war in Europe— navy peacoats, khaki stocking caps covering the whole head, wool turtleneck sweaters, and stories. How Norwegians helped Jews and other refugees escape from the Nazis, carrying them on skis over the mountains to secret boats and the safety of England.

One cold night older brother was late coming back from skiing the hills outside of town. As the temperature fell below zero father and I strapped on our skis, thinking of broken legs, frostbite and worse—unspoken of course. We met him at the edge of the woods. He lost track of time, then lost his way when the night closed like a closet door.

We didn't call it cross-country skiing, but that's a good name if it helps people do it. We just liked to get out in the woods away from crowds, make our own trails. Now when I ski with my family high in the Jemez Mountains, I tell my kids about grandpa and my first pair of skis. For my fiftieth birthday Mona gave me a pair of touring skis, laminated wood, made in Norway.

Changing Times

Just last year we loitered in overalls in downtown Omaha
    green corn running out of our ears, a pig in every pot.

Just last week we could look the grocer in the eye
    pay our bills on time, leave the back door unlocked.

Just yesterday we knew the neighbors by name,
    we could fetch the Sunday paper in our skivvies.

Today it is gurus and granola, trekking in Nepal.
    photographs of the hermit in front of his cave.

Like wall sockets, people waiting to be plugged in,
    investing with Christ on primetime TV.

Couples doing aerobics to their favorite hymns.
    PCs, DVDs, LCDs, if it costs money it's good for you.

Mother at Ninety

The sky is a blue canopy over Minnesota
    as I fly to Minneapolis from New Mexico.

Below are patches of green corn and hundreds of lakes
    like a chorus of blue eyes staring into the heavens.

I think of my aged mother in a St. Paul nursing home,
    where everyone is napping by late morning.

Strapped into wheelchairs and stretchers,
    tucked into their bodies like birds in winter.

Puffy heads like balls of cotton droop into their laps,
    a pinkish skin laced with purple veins.

Mother is down a hallway smelling of antiseptic and soap
    in a small room. A bed, chair, a few knickknacks.

Her life has been squeezed into a tube of toothpaste
    as she slowly moves to the edge of existence.

Once the Northland was the home of Vikings and mother
    a Valkyrie riding a horse with flaming nostrils to Valhalla.

She has outlived her generation. Winds of loneliness have
    worn her down to a smooth, white stone.

As if the video were rewinding, the circle of ripples in reverse
back to the original pebble dropped in a pond.

She speaks to me out of hollow eyes acquainted with death.
Why am I alive? She asks. There is no easy answer.

It is time for bone to loosen from bone, for blood to drain
away. Time for another journey, for the spirit to float free.

Handkerchief

Today when I wiped Maia's face with my handkerchief before
she went into school, I remembered my father doing the same thing
for me, and tears came to my eyes.

He'd wet the cloth with his tongue, lean over close and clean
the chocolate from the edges of my mouth.

As I become my father I cannot bear the thought of his death
and the dark side of time.

I wonder whether on some future day Maia will pause on the
steps of an elementary school and reach into the shadows of our
past with a handkerchief.

Night Song

When I was college age and oblivious, death
lingered at my grandfather's grave, like a distant
relation winking at kids from across the room.

Forty years later, he hangs out just up the street,
behind fences and mud walls, merging at dusk
like dark stains on the driveway.

I've caught the slouch of his drab colors turning
a corner, down an alley. The gray sagging folds
of his lips, the smell of metal filings and burnt oil.

Briefly, I thought he was next door—three cats
died from cancer, a snake, two hamsters and a bird.
Wilt for house plants. We changed our locks.

He was lurking in the crowd at my father's funeral,
smudges on the window panes when Maia was so sick.
Either he is bolder or my eye is clearer.

Squinting, I could almost see him sitting casual
on mother's bed in the nursing home. His voice like
dried grass and winter wind at the cemetery.

No surprises now when the glue comes unstuck—
bugs have turned the garden leaves into lace.
Sirens of police and rescue sing to me at night.

II ❖ First Taste of Mexico

We had several reasons for leaving the United States in 1968 and moving to Mexico for a year, but essentially it was the war in Vietnam, a war that was destroying people involved in a civil war 10,000 miles away, and poisoning our society at home.

Like many citizens north of the border, we were largely ignorant about Mexico, its history, geography, and culture, the fact that our tongues would wrap around us like a torn sheet, almost useless at times. Many adventures lay ahead.

We loaded an old one-wheel trailer and Volvo station wagon: two kids, two cats, pots, pans, bedding, dishes, typewriter, and books. We were barely out of Albuquerque driving south when a car pulled alongside and indicated that we had lost something. An aluminum box of goods had fallen off the roof rack; strangers had picked it up and raced to catch up to us. A positive omen. In fact, we needed and welcomed the gracious assistance of people throughout the year. I became obsessed with ropes, bungee cords, and tie-downs—items that might hold our lives together.

In Truth or Consequences we finally found someone on a Sunday to weld our exhaust system back together. Feeling that our progress was hardly faster than the earlier covered wagons, I wondered whether we would ever make it all the way to Guadalajara, Mexico.

After consulting a map we naively chose the road along the west coast, fantasizing about marine breezes and romantic views of the Sea of Cortés. A major mistake! The coast road frequently goes inland where it is hot and humid—no breeze, no dolphins in the distance. The coolest route to Guadalajara in August is the highland road through El Paso, right down the Chihuahuan plateau in the middle of the country.

We drove along for many miles south of the border before we could identify something strange about the scenery—no billboards. Where were the billboards? There were few road signs of any kind. Without them we were left completely on our own, as if we were looking at a landscape for the first time. Mexico was a foreign country.

The Gift

Two hundred miles south of the border is Hermosillo, capital of Sonora. A full day's journey for our old Volvo and trailer stuffed with kids, pets, utensils, and dreams about a Mexican refuge.

We were used to billboards, name brands, and meat wrapped in cellophane—some discretion and distance. Mexico is face-to-face, demanding attention—dead animals on the highway, bicycles and burros. Poor, dusty villages overflowing with kids and expectations. Men and women waiting like statues at the bus stop. Markets that smell like food.

All day the desert blew through the open car windows, a fine sandpaper rubbing away routines. By late afternoon, we felt empty and anxious on this first trip into Mexico, our first in a foreign country.

The Bugambilia Motel was an oasis—heavy, wooden furniture, blue and cream Talavera tile, and swimming pool. Gradually, the wheels stopped turning, the hot wind climbed back into the acacia trees.

With our beginner's Spanish, we could order four things for dinner. It was a *pollo frito* night. Halfway through the meal, baby Sarah's world collapsed—too many miles in a diaper on top of sacks and duffels. Too much heat shimmering over the asphalt. Where was her highchair? Where was her own bed?

She began with the weary blues, and then, as if feeding off her own sadness, she stretched her misery into a wail. Mona picked her up to go back to our room.

Just outside the door, they met an old campesino returning from the fields. Silvery stubble punctuated a dark, weathered face, a shock of white hair crowned his head. Seeing Sarah's distress, he quickly pulled some shell and cocoon rattles from his pack and tied them around his legs and arms.

Then he began to dance, bending and swaying to his own music. Ordinary clock time stopped as he slowly circled mother and child. At some point, Sarah's tears dried up, the clouds parted, and the gods of the desert were forgiven.

Her toothy laughter was sunshine and tonic for the old peasant's heart. He lightly touched her blonde head and vanished into the twilight.

Our first night, our first gift—a blessing from a Mexican dervish, who certainly continues to dance, if not in this world, the next.

One-Wheel Trailer

Earlier that month a hurricane had washed out the bridges along the Mexican coast. One of the bridges had its internal structure intact, but was missing the surface pavement. Cars and trucks could creep across on two rows of planks that spanned the eight or nine wooden cross members. But nothing was provided for my single trailer tire that ran in between.

Laughing workmen waved us on while a bus on our tail laid on its horn. I broke into a sweat and eased the trailer off the first cross member unto steel tie-rods sticking upward like spears, then up unto a wooden beam, and down again on the next batch of rods. At any moment I expected to hear the loud pop of a tire, exploding like a pricked balloon. I didn't have a spare, but the god of Goodyear rubber looked kindly on us.

Sopa

After a long day on Mexican roads, we longed for a quiet meal in Navajoa, but my Spanish caused a wrinkle in the menu. I asked the waiter whether the onion soup was made from milk, "*Es la sopa de cebolla con leche?*"

"*Con leche?*" A cloud settled over his face. He led me back to the kitchen describing in a blur of sound the ingredients of this savory soup. The exact recipe fell between us like so much sawdust on the floor.

A question of culture brought both of us to the kettle of soup, where we stirred it with a long ladle, as if we were witches choosing between the dried tongues of spiders and pickled eyes of newt.

The situation demanded resolution. At stake were issues of hospitality and national pride—the possibility of yet another bewildering question from a gringo. We needed to take the evening by the hand and lead it back to a table chirping with children, tostadas and bottles of Tecate.

I remembered the word for cream, *crema,* and suggested it. "*Sí, sí con crema,*" the waiter replied, relieved that harmony in the cosmos was restored. The pot of soup that had tilted over the abyss, now had two countries embracing it.

Tourist

At a campground along the coast, a tourist in a motor home
asked me how long we intended to stay in Guadalajara.
I said nine months. He looked surprised and reached for his
guidebook like a Baptist might retrieve his Bible: "Lookee here!"
he said, opening its pages. "There're only *six* things to see in
Guadalajara! We did it in a week."

Bilingual Means Having Two Tongues

For weeks I felt smaller and tame, as if Spanish had finally cut me down to size. Catching a few isolated nouns and phrases, most conversations collapsed to the sidewalk.

I listened to the cadence of speech, the rise and fall of families, the tempo of sirens, women gathering their children like hens or bargaining in the market. The heated exchange of oranges at the fruit stand fell down on my head like warm cinders.

I had always used my mouth like the white cane of a blind man, probing the neighborhoods with small choruses of How's the baby, Nice day, Where'd you get your flax seed? Bits of chit-chat laying down a trail like Hansel and Gretel. Neighbors wrapping words around friends.

But in Mexico, I went blank over the phone, searching for the smallest inkling to humble the wire. I yearned for an overcoat with oversized pockets stuffed with words. If I could only expose myself and discover the miracle of a second tongue.

Products replaced talk, labels that haunt the American around the globe: Coca-Cola, corn flakes, Aunt Jemima, Kodak. I would hold out a handful of change and let the seller pick and choose, while young men carried tin buckets of cement on their heads up three stories, building the supermarket, chattering away as if they understood each other.

Processional

The deep throat of a drum called me into the night streets of
Guadalajara. Beginning its feast day, a congregation was circling the
parish, led by a three-foot figure of Santa Teresita, a doll in white
silk on a platform of purple velvet. Her small arms stretched outward
as if sensing a direct communication from heaven, while blessing
her followers.

Mothers and sisters in Sunday clothes carried sleeping babies and
sang hymns. Teenagers ran ahead shooting bottle rockets into the
faithful. At the rear, a portly priest in black robes used a megaphone
to preach against sin: *pecado mortal, pecado contranatural,* and *pecado
venial.* No one paid any attention to warnings that slithered like
snakes down the street in front of him.

The mass was in a church with pictures of saints outlined in red
and blue neon. Afterwards crowds emptied into streets lined with
game and food booths, flying pink and yellow streamers. A demonic
maestro lit a castillo of fireworks thirty feet tall. He darted about
lighting string after string of bangs and pops. Pinwheels of firecrackers
flew into crowds, who stamped on the sparks. Finally the very top of
a pole spun and exploded, white ash and smoke scattered over the area.
The church bells rang and people wandered home.

Lingering in the shadows, I marveled at this mixture of ritual and
carnival. Midwestern fathers had not prepared me for Mexico. Turning,
I saw Lupe, a dark Indian, our new maid and baby-sitter. She held the
arm of a frail and withered figure, who shuffled a few steps, stopped.
Then a few more steps, uncertain of any real connection to the street.

Lupe smiled, presented me to her mother, and I gazed into a nut-
brown, wrinkled face that receded into the black hole of her shawl.
This woman, defined as much by absence as by flesh and blood,
lingered on some threshold. Like all ageless widows who transcend
both sin and redemption, she bore witness to the immutable mystery
of passing from this life to the next.

Tlaquepaque

We rented a house in Tlaquepaque, the cobblestones
    swept clean in the first light by old women in rebozos.
Lean bitches nosed the garbage collected on corners,
    picked up by drunks from the jail. Coat hangers held
their truck together. Rattle-trap buses roamed the corridors
    of the town, shaking it into dust.

The brazen bells of two heavy churches, a block apart,
    cracked open the morning.
The street overflowed with Sunday services, coco vendors,
    white slices of jícama brushed with chili.
Bodies floated into view, blessed sinners with breasts
    tied in ribbons and strawberry hats.

The air thickened with slices of orange. Peddlers in doorways
    sold small piles of blackened peanuts.
The smell of bananas from a warehouse three blocks away and
    urine from the alley.
Beneath the stained glass windows of the church, *borrachos*
    had pissed a deep pocket in the wall.

Evenings the mariachis called for a Mexican opera. The click
    of sequined heels, the snap of fingers.
The plaza filled with dark beauties in hoopskirts, wives
    flowered into lace mantillas.
Muchachos and muchachas slowly circled in opposite directions,
    el paseo. Searching for *un novio, una novia.*

In the shadows stood unforgiving fathers with gold watches for eyes.
    Anything was possible, friends might become lovers.

Marias

Beggars have been outlawed, but not poverty. The voices of children pulled at my arm—small noses and eyes oozed like thick cream. We had no suburbs to retreat to, no picket fences to hide behind.

The diminutive Indian mothers, who beg barefoot in Mexican cities, are called *Marias.* One baby slung in a rebozo, toddlers dozing on the sidewalk. Mona always finds some change for these unlikely Madonnas.

A middle-class Mexican told us to avoid charity, that many beggars have small farms outside town with pigs and chickens. The same excuse is used for panhandlers in New York City.

A mother and child found their way to our steel door in Tlaquepaque when we barely knew the way ourselves. Black bars covered the windows.

She opened her rebozo to a sick infant, skin like a mauve-colored condom pulled tight over the bones of a tiny bird. The mother's eyes asked me, Can you do something?

This Maria touched the desperate edge, like standing alone while a crowd rushes by. My own skin hung on me in folds, as if I were continually sitting down to eat.

Beyond a few coins, some scraps of food, I felt helpless, unable to explain the fat fruit rats in the *mercado,* the well-fed Franciscans in the cathedral. My tongue grew stiff in my throat.

With so much to forget, I seemed to understand less each day. Like the war in Vietnam, there were no answers, only the streets filled with the passion of mortality. Questions rattled the bed at night.

El Dia del Muerto

I

Three blocks east of the plaza is Rosas,
    no funeral too large, no service too small.
Open day and night week in, week out.
Ashes on the tile floor, pea green walls
    an aged stuffed chair for waiting.

2

Tito's mother accidentally killed two of her children—
    she was uptight, her lover was late.
Refugio's oldest fell down a well uncovered in the backyard.
Jorge, not yet two, swallowed some rat poison, was fatally
    bitten, caught a deadly virus—it's not clear.

3

All Hallow's Eve, on the Parián—Tlaquepaque's central plaza.
    A campesino and I watched the local borrachos dancing with
    brooms and wives. His strong face seasoned by work in the fields.
I asked about his work, family. He was proud of his seven sons.
    No daughters? I asked.
He described a two-year-old daughter—brain damaged—hospitalized
    for three months before dying. Medical costs of some *treinta mille*
    pesos—about $2,400. But he paid it all off, *poca a poco.*
He pulled out a small Kodak slide from his wallet, held it to the light.
    There was his dead daughter, lying like a statue on blue velvet.
Replacing the slide, he got up, shook my hand and reset his hat for walking
    into the darkness. His eyes like two weathered oaks in a storm.

4

Shelves cover the walls in Rosas,
    caskets floor to ceiling.
Most are white, short,
    three to four feet long.
Both plain and scrolled in gold,
    with and without handles.

A Machete for Thorn and Prickly Pear

(FOR PETER)

Explorers in a strange world, son Peter and I hiked the barranca at
the edge of Guadalajara, slashing its course through the countryside.
Small banana plantations at the bottom, then up to a rocky hilltop
overlooking grain fields, scattered beneath us like pieces of quilt.

We stood there in a stubbled field, distant from village or road.
Peasant families bent to the earth as if poised for an ageless painting.
Lean muscular arms cut the corn, an abundance falling to the ground.

Men loaded the gray burro high and heavy with yellow stalks.
A woman with black braids brought water in a clay pot, a rope
slung around her forehead. Another woman strained at ropes across
her chest, lugging a load of charcoal to the next village. A burro
dragged two ponderous logs out of the mountains to Uruapan,
seven kilometers away. Thousands of small fish sun-dried on the
road from Chapala to Jocótepec.

This place, barely visible from a distance, was all shades of
brown, mixed with the dusty gray-green of sage, mesquite, and
agave. But how to evoke the quiet of a landscape filtered through
the thin winter sun, broken only by faint breezes and the clatter
of birds—that dry quiescence of late harvest.

A campesino strode out of the brush on a path worn plain
by huaraches. A simple greeting with an innate sense of courtesy.
He appeared from nowhere, only to fade at the bend in the path,
past the hacienda razed by Pancho Villa, past the revolution in
Orozco's murals—Father Hidalgo with a flaming torch burning
away the bondage of the oppressed—Freedom and Land for
Indian and mestizo, barely visible now in the weeds.

We turned towards home, feeling we had walked backwards in
time, had witnessed a tableau—peasants who for ages worked the
fields from sunup to sundown. The light quickly surrendered to
the dark. On the horizon cars and buses rushed to the next city.

Face to Face

A leper sat in the center of the main plaza, on the shortest route from home to tortillaria. Half of his face was purple jelly, as if one cheek had begun to melt and drift back towards the ear.

I was acquainted with leprosy, my grandfather had sent money to a leprosarium in India, and the Santal Mission sent us photos of ulcerated skin, hands without fingers, faces with half a nose. Nevertheless, I avoided any direct encounter and detoured around him.

Finally one morning, I walked up to the leper, looked straight at him, and said, "*Buenos días.*" From a small, dark opening used for a mouth, a distinctly human voice whispered back, "*Buenos días.*" A wrinkled hand reached out to shake one of mine.

Day before Christmas

In the chill of early morning, garbagemen and I laughed at my old fashioned suit coat, pulled up to my ears. The cathedral's twin steeples turned pink, the elegant fronds of the palm trees were silver in the first light.

Blue and white buses rumbled like bass drums over the cobblestones. A banquet of smells floated from the vendors on the plaza. Cinnamon and sugar churros, baked sweet potatoes, chile and tacos. Cobs of buttered corn roasted on charcoal grills.

In a chorus of horns and bleats, the old goat man chased his herd across the intersection, waving a stick and shouting *"Putas! Putas!"*

Yawning and stretching, this day had such promise, something wonderful would happen.

The young Eduardo called to me from across the street. With his crippled leg, he half-hopped and skipped—his good leg did double-duty. Together we walked quickly to show he was equal to any kid his size.

He guided me to special shops with special prices for me at Christmas time. Glassware and onyx chessboards, clay purple pigs tucked in corners. Rooster and toro piñatas swung from the ceiling.

At last he led me to the *Nacimiento* in the central square. Life-size statues of Mary and Joseph had been kneeling there for weeks. So patiently, surrounded by sheep, burros and shepherds—waiting as Mexico itself waits, for the conversion of pain and suffering into peace and prosperity.

Eduardo pointed to the manger covered with lace that shimmered like spun gold. He pulled at my arm so I would bend over, and whispered in my ear, as if anticipating a marvel. Tomorrow morning, he said, holding tight to my hand. *En la mañana,* the crib will no longer be empty. *El Niño Jesús,* he said, and his eyes grew large and shiny like two ornaments.

Eduardo didn't understand that for me *la milagro,* the miracle, had already happened.

Jesús (Jesse) Chavez and Neighbors

A tired sensuality clung to Jesse, as if he had just untangled himself from the arms and scented breasts of his lover.

He said he was married to Fama, who said she was the widow of a United States general. Fama lived in Washington, D.C., but twice yearly came to Guadalajara to ride in the taxi she had bought for Jesse.

He specialized in tours to Lake Chapala, restaurants and shops that tipped him under the counter for bringing in customers. American tourists trusted him because he spoke English.

Jesse would look into the sky and say, "In the long run, it pays to be honest. There are two hundred million people in the States. I want business from only one percent."

Dick and Jim lived in the apartment below Jesse on Avenida Vallarta. Dick's father, a steel magnate in Chicago, had recommended to Dick that he live in Mexico with his good friend Jim—father would pay for it. The American way.

Jim was thin and fastidious, forever arranging the apartment, as he did his life. Dick spoke Spanish, was well built, steady and quiet. They loved to entertain.

When Jim's parents came for their first visit south of the border, Jim cleaned and shopped a whole week prior to their arrival on Sunday morning.

On Saturday night, Jesse went out to celebrate his birthday. He brought back a mariachi band, knocked at Dick's and Jim's apartment, invited himself and the band inside.

The band played and ate, ate and played—all the fancy food, all the polished apples and oranges, chips and salsa, fancy meats and breads—all the chocolates and mints.

Growing tired, Jesse climbed to the roof of the building, fired his pistol three times into the sky, and went to bed—one more year.

Towards dawn, the exhausted band left, charging Jim and Dick for all their songs and serenading. Jim could not mention Jesse's name without stuttering.

Nuevo Laredo

We had driven from our house in Tlaquepaque to the airport in Laredo.
A Texas ranger caressed his obscene six-shooter in the lobby. Father
and mother were coming to Mexico for a visit.

Dozens of Americanos sat patiently in chairs or stood in a long line, waiting
to get tourist cards and auto papers in Nuevo Laredo's customs building
just over the border in Mexico. It might take hours.

My parents were elderly and we needed to reach Guanajuato that evening.
I took the documents for six of us, placed several dollars on top—
discreet, but visible—and walked to the front of the line.

I said, *Dispénseme*—"excuse me"—to the tourist being served, and *Buenos
días, señor* to the border official, dressed in a neat, green uniform.
I gave him our papers.

He carefully laid aside the other person's forms and processed ours, smiled
and wished me *Buen viaje*—a good trip—and we were on our way.
It took less than five minutes.

Back in the car, a few miles down the highway, mother remarked, Wasn't it
nice of the Mexican official!? He must have known we were in a hurry.
I agreed with her.

This Is a Cup

On the first day of her Mexican holiday, mother, with her matronly manner, gave an English lesson to our teenage maid. She held a cup in front of Felícitas, and repeated the words, "This is a *cup*."

Her voice slowly rose in pitch and stress as she suspended the object in front of her, like a reward for finally articulating "cup." The maid's face clouded over as if she were caught in a storm.

Like many tourists, mother assumed she spoke the parent Ur-language, with which she might save at least one Mexican. To pierce the veil of peasantry and force English to emerge from the depths of her student's genetic files.

At another level it was not linguistics, but a question of character, as if mother embodied Nordic virtue, the imposition of will on the otherwise passive, largely pagan, surface of reality.

Her lesson represented the right of conquest, like Columbus gathering a group of West Indians for morning recitation: "This is a cross! Where is your gold? This is a cross!"

Like the conquistadors, mother felt the righteousness of God— not as a familiar, but as a stern father who loves and corrects his children in spite of himself.

One Afternoon in Tlaquepaque

The adobe wall holding in the church was solid
and steadfast. A web ringing the compound.
Peasants tipped their hats at the iron gate.

Mornings two ancient women crossed to the wall,
sold oranges in the shadows, peddled gum and
sodas, candy for children on the longest way home.

Evenings they returned to two straw mats, slept
in a windowless stairwell. Like chaff,
life danced endlessly along this street.

It took a bus careening into that wall
the afternoon broken into pieces of adobe.
The wrinkled women no longer hidden in rebozos.

I too depended on the wall, led by it to the plaza
our feet wedded to an old pathway,
drawn there waiting for the dust to sing.

But a bus missed the corner, the brakes failed,
forcing a new passage.
Dark patches of blood soaked dry in the rubble.

Neighbors gathered there for the miracle
the place where the bus had touched us.
It was why we examined the remains of the wall.

Not using the word for death, *muerto*, we whispered
    with lowered heads, assuming that space itself
like time had somehow been severed.

We searched for that moment turning a corner,
    a crack to slip through with the women.

III ⊞ Borderlands

Ages ago people began to settle in the borderlands of the
Southwest, where mesas and mountains meet, where deep
clefts are cut into the desert. This tableland of mesquite and
juniper stretches more than four hundred miles to the south,
from Albuquerque across the border to Chihuahua, and
beyond. It is framed by the tawny ridges of mountains, like
the undulating spine of a dinosaur.

Such places of extremes have traditionally been the
spawning grounds of prophets and religion. For centuries,
wanderers have fled the common way and sought the refuge
of this sun-bleached region, following ghosts that rise like
dust devils from the sand. In the seeming emptiness of the
desert, spirits are free to roam, free to invade the imagination.

Ever since World War II, with the development of a
nuclear bomb at Los Alamos, New Mexico has been caught
between past and future, undecided whether to ride the
high-tech revolution to affluence, build condos and shopping
centers, or quietly retreat down an acequia to a small
vegetable garden, to dream about a simpler time before the
invasion of machines and pollution.

⊞

Albuquerque's Mt. Calvary Cemetery

Just outside Mt. Calvary to the east is another cemetery, where
    green gives way to desert. The graves are mounds of gravel
    above ground, as if the hole were a vessel pulled over the body.

Most of the markers are missing, a few broken crosses of white
    pipe. No guardian, not a tree—nothing to center this place, the
    way in and out, the pathway to the next world.

It is called an abandoned potter's field, but two identical graves
    are recent—yellow-painted rocks, plastic roses, a garland of snow.
    A eulogy for someone's parents? Children certainly—somebody's.

I met an old Indian there. He'd been chopping wood in the drainage
    ditch, like a coyote moving into the suburbs. The logs on his wagon
    were tied up with electric cord and he stopped to talk.

With strange words like the humming of the interstate, he pointed to
    the mountain with its nuclear arsenal, slowly turned in a circle to
    city-center, the homeless living under the Rio Grande bridge.

Was he the caretaker, two copper coins for eyes? Should I have paid
    him? He made me wonder why the dead could be outside the fence—
    or even inside. Mt. Calvary is surrounded by cemetery.

Jemez Mountains

(FOR BOB)

Miles into the mountains foraging for wood
    the weather changed from snow to cobalt
        sky and back again.

Leaving a flabby city
    to drive a wedge into oak or piñon
        deadfalls with winter

Bones, brittle dry.
    Such abundance
        cut by hand against the cold.

As the last storm shutdown the forest
    we could look under it, out over the valley
        as if from a cave.

Clouds catching the light, a profusion
    of ruby feathers
        danced across the mesa.

For a few moments autumn turned around
    trapped in a tunnel, the eye
        at both ends.

Then with the patter of aspen leaves
    the air grew thick and white
        with tiny stars.

Door-to-Door Chile

Alfonso came to the front door peddling September sunshine and a bumper crop: "Hatch green chile," he said with a warm, harvest voice, "just picked yesterday." His face glowed with good news, as if he were announcing the winner of a national lottery. Indeed, with green chile everyone is a winner, and, oh, so reasonable.

Instead of the sauna, birch twigs and snow baths, ancient Mexicans cultivated the chile pepper. And for the aficionado who likes his food dancing with green flames, Hatch green chile and New Mexico are like Vienna Sausage and Austria, Roquefort and France.

From hardy stem to elegant tip, this green elongated pod hangs on a squat bush looking innocent. Like a beach boy in a bikini, the torso and thighs of the chile soak up fire from the sun all summer, storing vitamin C and virility for the winter.

Chile is addictive. Most New Mexicans have chile for breakfast, then spend the rest of the day looking for excuses to eat more of it. Cans of chile tucked in luggage for travel abroad. Cases of Old El Paso are shipped to exiled New Mexicans around the globe.

So when I told Alfonso, "No thanks," he shook his furrowed brow. Had I misunderstood, was I a bit loco perhaps? Had we somehow been exiled to Minnesota or Maine?

I thought of another peddler selling the last pickings of citrus from Mesa, Arizona. He reminded me that frost had wiped out the Texas crop. Never mind that the grapefruit were bitter and the oranges hard like weapons. Gesturing with his palms open to fickle fate, it was *not* his fault.

But this was the cream-of-the-crop Hatch chile, not the dregs of citrus. With rounded shoulders Alfonso carried this strange heresy to his truck. Then he shook it off with a smile that restored the planets to their orbits, "Another time, perhaps. I'll come back."

"Please come back," I said, "I'm bound to come to my senses."

February in New Mexico

I know spring has come too soon
    when young couples sink to the grass
        hang on each other's lips, feeling
            more than ashes below the waist.

It's a serious problem in the Sunbelt—
    not knowing the right season for love or
        death, when to sharpen the scythe,
            when to break all the plates.

Look at California, surfing with Beach Boys,
    an endless trip through a wet tunnel.
        Mature men devoted to the ultimate wave,
            forgetting that salmon die after spawning.

First Love

She's the only one
    he allows on his motorbike
        and she knows it.

Something older
    than her fourteen years
        tells her how to toss her head.

Her bewitching brown hair
    tumbles like a waterfall
        down her back

You can see the new moon
    in her smile
        as they drive past.

The City Limits

New Mexico has crept into Albuquerque.
    I found pigweed and thistle in the jagged
    cracks of the parking lot.

Last night mule deer from Bear Canyon
    ate the spinach and Swiss chard.
    A skunk family lives under Bel Air School.

Just when we thought we had a handle
    on civilization, we find desert on both sides
    of the city limits.

Like that kid who hears about dust to dust
    at a funeral, looks under his bed and shouts,
    "Oh, oh! Someone is either coming or going!"

Collecting: A Modern Paradigm

This is the time to collect things, to get into collecting. We are moving beyond Thoreau's lean vision, that parsimonious prophet of New England. We're not afraid of money or goods, treating them like excrement, a guilty thing out of sight in banks or privies.

Right and left, liberal and conservative, young and old have joined the antique road show. People into health foods, meditation, and yoga. Have money, dividends, have angels in the east. Reality is Maya, an illusory market played with credit cards and ATMs. Zen masters own stocks. Gurus and evangelists fly to all parts of the globe to sit and invest.

The old message was Get rid of possessions, trim to essentials, sandals, and begging bowl. Give what you have to the poor. Without things you are free. The revolutionary and saint travel light.

The prophet in the crystal cathedral preaches accumulation. God's grace measured by wealth. Freedom is possession. You can travel with things, on and in things. Goods can be stored. Possessions provide a point of view, a sense of history, plans for the future.

No more bourgeois guilt. What's the difference between dishwashers and Tai Chi, trips to Esalen, karate, and snowmobiles? Lion's club, Elks, Masons, talking to dolphins and whales, teepees, trail bikes, organic figs?

Most stores today are toy stores, boats in desert driveways, SUVs for wilderness. Stereos, hookahs, swimming pools, yogurt makers, carrot juicers, Adelle Davis. Rooms for meditation and massage, pool tables, swing sets, herbs by Rodale, TVs for kitchen and bath, hiking boots, mummy bags and skis.

A friend collects books, stacks them on the floor like a labyrinth. Students collect grades, degrees, each other. Husbands collect wives, children, retirement. Landlords and rent, lawyers and fees, detectives and evidence, churches and tithes. Stamps, taxes, coins, and guns.

The one crisis is storage space. Two-car garages are full, add-on rooms are full. I built a shed a year ago, it's full. Odd pieces of wood, three tents, bits of electric cord, four tarps, badminton set, three boogie boards, bent wickers from a broken croquet set, cans of paint, lamp fixtures, fuses, new and used nails, and screws.

You're either a collector or something collected. Things are the meeting ground of culture and counterculture, of Republican and Democrat, Christian and Muslim. And who knows, when we're totally displaced by our own junk, we might meet each other at the top of the heap.

Sarah's Songs

Sarah, four years old, sings her songs to her delighted sister, Maia, five months old. She plunks a broken, plastic ukulele creating her songs as she leafs through picture books. After each song she circles Maia blowing on a plastic harmonica.

I

Oh the lizard, the blue lizard
     Oh yah
Meets a lizard on another page
     Oh yah
They're on a big rock
They're on the road
     Oh yah
On the road, on their way to town
     Oh yah

II

Oh Herod, King Herod was terrible
     Oh Herod was a terrible man.
          Oh yah.
He killed the children
     All the children.
          Oh yah.
And Baby Jesus, oh Baby Jesus
     Went to Egypt, far from Herod
          Oh yah.
He saw the pyramids in the desert
     And became a boy.
          Oh yah.

Grandfather Tree

One evening in mid-December, he looked out and was amazed to see the family car drive up with a tree tied to its roof. A bristly tree—about eight feet tall—was brought like an intruder through the front door into the living room.

Different from other trees that drop their leaves in the fall, this was an evergreen. At the ends of its branches, tiny points of sap oozed from needles and glistened like droplets of sperm.

Since before the Vikings, when the sun ran away to the south and winter grew dark like a cave, his ancestors brought green trees into their houses.

The smell of resin drifted into the bedroom. Mornings it was like waking up in the mountains.

He spent many sleepless nights talking to the tree and the tree seemed to respond, like a small wind causing it to shudder.

Touching the trunk, he sensed that the tree had roots that descended into the basement, into the earth below. Underground the roots twined north to Minnesota, and north again—under the primordial ice—to Norway.

Although this tree was cut and slowly dying, he felt something fresh inside, as if a warm current flowed out of the boughs through his arms, and into that round cavity below his chest. It tingled like putting cold hands into a pan of warm water. It filled him up, like eating a bowl of oatmeal with brown sugar when icicles grow from the roof.

The old tomcat—who never did such things in the house— took to squirting the base of the tree, as if he were falling in love. He batted at the shiny glass balls, a few fell to the floor and shattered like a sunset bouncing off water.

The world was tilting at a different angle. November had been yellow and brown, but after the tree arrived, the house began to feel green. Invisible blades of grass were sprouting from the wood floors.

One night after dark, the family gathered around this tree, covered with small white candles that radiated like a children's choir filling the room with song. On the top of the tree was a small silver star, where the roof opened to the moon glowing in a purple sky.

They held hands all around. And behind them, emerging from the lingering shadows, were their parents and grandparents—*bestemoren* and *bestefaren*—one generation after another, like ripples on a pond. Everyone, all the relations, slowly circled that miraculous tree and sang the solstice song:

> *The world will come green again,*
> *Everything will green again.*

Winter in Atlantic City 1970

This is the off-season, yet people carry on as if it were a
real city. Nerves are shot, only skin and bones remain from
overexposure—the burden of fashion attire. Any stranger
can drive in this time of year, shop in a drugstore, see a movie,
leave without question.

Early morning the boardwalk is bare, storefronts drink in
the cold mist. "Don't litter" says a bag worn by an old relic
pushing three frozen dog turds into the sand with a newspaper.
Some stores had winter sales before closing, some are only half
open, hibernating, filled with junk from around the world.

The sun is thin as I walk the beach covered with shells
and rotting fish. The storm last night heaped mounds of
long-neck clams high on the sand—they sound like a chorus
of false teeth, chattering and stretching their necks, probing
the air, longing for the waterline. Then back into their shells.
One by one they fall silent.

The diving horse winters down south, the funny house
is boarded up. If only the beach with its line of brown scum
could be rolled up until spring. They're adding to Convention
Hall for bigger Miss Americas. The eternal flame for John F.
Kennedy is out, his plastic wreath tipped over. The show
begins again in June.

Thomas Watson got food poisoning at the White Tower
hamburger joint, I leave my french fries on the plate. At
Gibberson's four fading widows sit over coffee, unraveling
their lives in lottery tickets.

"Night Elaine," they say to the waitress.

"See you in the morning," she returns.

"Not me," responds a feathered hat, "I'm going to
    Miami tomorrow; ten days. It's a nice thing,
    you know."

En route to my room, I pass the gnarled, black scrub lady
sucking on a cigarette. She guards the linen closet like a dark
spirit hovering over a fallen world—all those sheets and
pillows soiled by people who have passed on.

This city is mostly memory, a shrine of somber relics.
A wrinkled dowager dreaming of childhood when mom
and dad brought her to the seashore.

Sitting on the World

*On my knees laying new tile in the kitchen. Held out my hand for a
scraper and a two-year-old waddled over and perched on it. For most
of her early life Maia has sat on me, climbed, or swung.*

I've been the swaying bridge over crocodile swamps
    the logs spanning the Royal Gorge.

With apples hanging from my ears Maia climbed
    a tree, to the watchtower on top.

On all fours I was a horse, then a camel—she shouted
    "Hut-hut!" crossing the Sahara.

Crossed legs became a teeter-totter, up and down, then
    onto my knee where she watched the sun set.

And we danced, almost from the beginning. Holding
    her on my hip we'd sway and bend.

Releasing my hand she'd lean far out and stretch her
    arms, barely missing coffee table and chair.

Clasped hands were a swing set, up into the sky with
    breathtaking twists. The audience applauded.

Not long ago I bent over at the refrigerator looking
    for leftovers when Maia threw herself on my back.

We wavered over an abyss, but the primal walkway held.
    She's getting too big for this and I am older.

Healing

Healing comes from behind
    even as you plot and plan
you hear the stream, its voice
    rising above the cars & clatter
in your head.

It washes right through the room,
    failures float away.
Pebbles and silt fill every crack
    the hard shell of a cactus
flowers.

Healing comes from behind
    turns your head around.
You drop your clothes to the floor
    step into the lustral stream
and bathe.

State Fair

(FOR MY FATHER)

I

Every year in September, they all come back again, the small towns, farms and ranches. Funneled into the fairgrounds, straight to the heart of Albuquerque.

The whole city stops to watch, kids' hands reach into dad's pockets—dad feels something spinning in the back of his head.

Right inside the gate are nubile girls, sequined and scented, twirling batons on the green and prancing like proud fillies.

Further on, the exhibits. In one block you can walk across the state and back again, through rows of blue-ribbon jams and pickles, wooden plows and solar converters, wander the dizzy edge between Navajo rugs and nuclear fusion, Angora rabbits and Discorama on the Midway.

There's a dry-your-own-fruits-and-vegetables demonstration of a live television flower show in the Floriculture, parimutuel, tag your tots, junior swine show with cutting horses and goats with real milk, judges like three scrawny turkeys under the grandstand with a miniature train plowing through Tom Bolack's republican Garden of Eden, with chiles as big as squash, and squash as big as watermelons.

FFA kids clutch their hands at the auction ring while their pet Hereford brings a down payment for college, across from the mouth with the ten-in-one gadget that slices, dices, crinkles, chops, turns a carrot into a carnation, leftovers into hash, just for mom and he'll throw in a whatsitz that peals, seals, and sharpens your fingers for free.

But I missed the gypsy woman at the Minnesota Fair, standing on a platform in front of astral signs. For two dollars, you could ask her for your name and your fortune. This modern sibyl would purr into her mike, "I believe it's John Hanson," he'd nod and she continued, "John, I sense you're having troubles with your in-laws."

He'd tuck his chin into his overalls. "Well, John, it'll work out just fine by the end of the month. Monday's your lucky day, five your lucky number."

I once snuck up close to her husband working the crowd, but didn't find any hidden wires. Somebody said they made enough in six months to winter in Florida. It was a bargain—advice like hers costs a lot more today.

2

After dark, great rivers of people flow along the streets, in and out of buildings. The air is sticky sweet with cotton candy, and they drift towards the Midway, feeling the excitement that comes from brushing against the tawdry and forbidden.

Midway to what or where? It's more than amusement, every game is carnal and every carney is cut from the same cloth, glazed eyes and a cigarette. As if sex were a dart game, a ball in the basket.

"Hey lucky. Win a big one! Lemme show ya how it's done!" This is finally a chance—who doesn't want to own the *big* one!

"Hey macho! Are you man enough to ring the bell with this hammer?"

Girls in monograms and tattoos hug their teddy bears, clutch the long-necked Mr. Pibb.

As a kid it seemed so innocent when I worked a week for a small carnival on Main Street. I got free passes on the rides and loose change for setting up the bottles filled with lead. Farm boys threw like the big leagues and lost.

What happened to the man with the hollow stomach? The guy with a dirty hanky around his mike wants to guess your age, whisper something nasty in your ear.

Have you seen the spider girl?
     She's alive.
Talk to her, she'll talk to you.
Don't expect to see her mate—
     she's a Black Widow you know.

It's all fakery and mirrors, a guise for the gullible. And yet, maybe the "freak" show is a peephole into the mystery itself, the Wizard of Oz before the unmasking.

Abuse of Drugs
Can Cause
This Madness
Delivers the Message
With Hammer Force

If Drugs Remove the Veil
Can You Face the Other Side?

A pair of teenagers are too stoned to read the signs on the tent. The attendant in dark glasses dabs at his rheumy nose. A cop slams an Indian against the back wall behind a booth, where players shoot water into a clown's mouth.

Dad and I used to walk up and down the Midway in St. Paul, past the girlie shows, while he searched for something decent. He thought the midget show was safe, like looking at ourselves in concave mirrors. Tempest Storm, the tiny stripper, wasn't even sexy. The announcer warned the leering boys in the front row that her bra might break or g-string snap. By the end it felt cheap, as if we had spent an evening hidden in our neighbor's closet or under his bed.

This year my daughter paid to see Pete Moore, the littlest man on earth. She talked to him, he talked back. Pete seemed happier than Ronnie and Donnie Galyon, the Siamese twins with one belly button, whose eyes were fixed in space.

"Hey there! The show's ready to start, it's showtime, don't be late!" The performer on the outside stage drew the sword out of his throat and walked inside. The big city barker winked, "You older fellows stick around! It's a different show after midnight."

3

Mel Lambert, the announcer from Salem, Oregon, filled time between bronc riding and steer wrestling: "In twenty-six years of working rodeo, I never heard Wilbur Plagett, the clown, tell an off-color, smutty joke."

A few years ago a bare-bronc rider flipped back over the horse's rear flank, flicked by a hoof, then crashed to the ground like a bag of bones. He broke his back, just like that—in the time a piece of lightning might crease you top to bottom.

When a bucking horse raced out of the arena, Mel shouted, "Get outta the way of this one—everyone 'cept hippies, that is!" Mel looked behind the chutes, "Oops, a long hair who'd forgot how to shave just bit the dust." The crowd laughed and clapped. All those folks with Stetsons and Tony Lama boots, the Star Spangled Banner in their eyes.

The West is still the country of the Lone Ranger, a white face with ruddy cheeks and neck. All that yearning for a simpler time, when you could just shoot a varmint without getting a phone call from PETA or the Sierra Club.

Once an Appaloosa with head down and flying mane rammed the wall and dropped dead, while the rider flew into the seats.

Where else can a man prove himself in an eight-second contest with an animal? The crowd sits waiting for the whine of the ambulance. This is what the wilderness has come to.

The Brahma bulls always come last, those monstrous humps, their balls like the clappers of a big bell, swinging to and fro. This event is older than cowboys, going back four thousand years to Crete and Asia Minor. Sacred boys and girls vaulted the head of the bull-god in an ultimate dance with fate.

Bull-riding is larger than a contest between bull and rider. Those mighty hooves shake the earth, he might kick out the lights. His horns might skewer the ladies in the front row.

One night at the rodeo, it felt like the bull against the coliseum, as if some primitive force were let loose. This monstrous creature might bring it all down, all the supermarkets, banks and power plants, all the polluters and hypocrites, the power and greed of drug companies, insurance, AMA, Gulf and Exxon. In that brief time, we took back our lives, took charge again, took hold of our bodies, felt them pulse with authority, tiny flames shot into all our limbs.

That's the bull and the bull dance. No winners and losers, just the fantastic surge of raw energy and a momentary vision, then the exhaustion, the clean emptiness inside as we carried the kids back to the car and drove home.

Connection

Last night it rained in Albuquerque.
  The East Fork of the Jemez, forty miles away
    is too muddy for fishing.

I thaw out some meat as mule deer move down
  into the canyons to feed, the buck sends the doe
    across the clearing first.

Red chile whirs in the blender and a cornice of
  snow cuts off the trail to Lake Katherine
    in the Pecos Wilderness.

It's this connection I want to make—not the leaky
  roof or faucet. Not even the need to move rabbit
    close to the house for winter.

The aspen are skinny old men flailing in the wind.
  The East Fork ices at the edges in the twilight
    while I cook stew in the kitchen.

Father and Daughter Backpacking

After farewell to Mona and Maia, our first backpacking trip. Daughter and I tramped into the Jemez Mountains, through the saddle of a butte, to the high ridges of Peralta Canyon. In a short time we were all alone and ready for adventure.

Lesson one—at ten years, Sarah grew discouraged carrying her pack when I walked ahead, setting the pace. Hence, frequent stops for snacks—Vienna sausages and trail mix. In the afternoon, she took the lead, fresh as springtime, and talked of getting her hiking legs. Me too.

Sanchez Canyon was dry for several miles and we needed water for a campsite. But shortly we came to a rivulet, then finally a tiny stream and a shallow pool. Almost primeval, sheltered by willow and sumac, just deep enough for bathing.

At home, my partner resisted getting out of bed, but here she was up at dawn making breakfast—oatmeal, raisins, bread and peanut butter, hot chocolate. We talked about the night, the spooky sounds, spirits all around us.

We explored the area like pioneers claiming a bit of the wilderness. The canyon wall was so steep we crept up on all fours. We planned an exit, if necessary. Flash floods had cleaned out a canyon in Colorado to the north, RVs swept away in a muddy torrent. We watched water skaters scoot along the surface, their oversized pads like tiny outriggers, reflected on the sandy bottom.

We tested our knives and each other, carving sticks, playing mumblety-peg on a stump. She knew without my saying that knives are important, more than useful. My father carried a small pocketknife, as do I. When Sarah first swam a length of the pool, we gave her a penknife as a prize.

We found the Big Dipper in the endless sky and our minds turned somersaults, how small we felt and how large. We learned to clear away the cobwebs of childhood, that father and daughter, daughter and father was a dance and we were just beginning.

Requiem on the Oregon Coast

(FOR PETER)

After setting up camp, Peter and I walked the beach.
    Long banks of clouds caught the dying light,
    as if the dark forces of night were triumphant,
    the sun sinking away in defeat.

For a moment I felt that shudder that comes to wanderers
    at sunset. Feeling abandoned we must face
    the shadows alone, see them float through our bodies
    like mist on the water.

Eight years old, Peter sensed the solemnity, the potential
    for surrender, and quietly said,
        "Dad, walk with dignity." He spoke from the heart
    and I knew I could count on him.

Rain in Albuquerque

Hot winds shriveled the corn. Fires
    in the mountains.
Even the prickly pear was wrinkled and limp.

Where are the monsoons? Then tonight
    a slow rain, slivers of white light
past the street lamp, the dog is confused.

We can actually smell again, juniper and yew.
    The wings of the Douglas fir lift and shake off
the dust, puffs of desert talcum.

I stand in the street with open face and palms
    like some feathered priest—Tlaloc, father of mists
a crown of yellow butterflies and heron feathers.

An ancient ceremony with four pitchers of water—
    thunder rocks the old woman, the heavens open.
A scroll of seeds spills from the deity's mouth.

In the saturated dark, the desert will bloom anew—
    toads and cicadas rejoice, while every grass
and limb quickens with a green flame.

End of Autumn

This is the autumnal cleansing: no tobacco, no smoke
    of any kind, no alcohol, heavy meats or stews.

Just simple grains and fruits, hot baths, travel by foot.
    Each day begins with the juice of two lemons.

It is the far side of harvest when pores turn into gold.
    Teeth ache for squash and pumpkin left in the field.

The dead and dying fill the granary, carrots are packed
    in sawdust, the sun barely crawls to the mountaintop.

I must shave the hair from my body, hang mistletoe
    from my breasts, a sprig of juniper for my pubis.

2

The other side of the harvest is the silver pod
    of the milkweed, the rattle of a dry pinecone.

Winter's white head drives him crazy, his crotch
    is smooth and cool.

With crops in every cavity, blood flows into clear
    ideas, we've a whole season to think.

My tongue is still, covered with wool, my breath
    a small cloud of vapor.

Trees strip down to the bone, black bears move
    into the guest house. The party is over.

Soon people will ride a brittle wind to the back
    of their heads. And lock the doors.

Roots

Sarah and I climb the thirsty mesa, find a deep pocket
    for a fire. Ghosts made of mesquite blow over our heads.

I lift an old nest of wire and twig to the wind.
    It sings and hums a higher spell than the power lines.

We search for some silent pageant. Pieces of rabbit fur
    are clotted with cat tracks and blood.

We must learn to read these relics—fossilized antlers, uncle's
    pocket watch, old oval photographs in the steamer trunk.

Ancestors are tiny bones that catch in the throat. Strange
    tongues—trolls and gnomes hide in the closet.

We are immigrants, the lost and found of every generation.
    Our roots grow lengthwise.

Winter

I

How easily we speak of death
    after the first frost.
Winter is such a relief.

All summer there were weeds
    insects and bugs
a dizzy hum after dark.

Children hoed the garden,
    so much must die
for the chosen seed.

Fruit was the family's
    victory, harvesting
another generation.

2

The crows arrive
    linger like souls
with unfinished business.

The strangest sounds come
    from the cat, feathers
caught in her throat.

We watch these birds
    like plump raisins
swinging in the trees.

Noisy, obnoxious
    their bellies an omen—
the sun migrates south.

3

One thing ends before another
    begins—a sacred rhythm.
Spring will come again and

Again after I'm dead, after
    all that is now living.
A simple circle the final lesson.

Anniversary

(FOR MONA)

1

Hardly a warrior, yet how many times
I've returned defeated, and your voice

pulled me through the long, blue tunnel.
You are a deep pool of water, and I seek

the quiet forbearance of a granite boulder.
Now it is my turn to stretch my arms

round the base of a tree, and watch you
climb to the next level of your brilliance.

2

We're not the stuff of theater or fantasy
but the sinuous fiber of words themselves,

as if survival depended on oral history.
We are those places where we merged,

placing our heart's hunger in each other's hands.
Always between us, the celebration of dream

half-remembered: a pole sunk into the earth,
the family tree radiant with branches.

Here, rub oil into our bodies, the dark wound.
Together, our souls have begun to flower.

IV ▦ On the Road

Where do you feel most alive? Is there a place where you feel such a deep sense of well-being that excitement runs through your veins like electricity, where you feel like dancing and making love at the same time? A place that knows you as well as you know it?

Some folks are rooted to a piece of earth, no matter how flat or cold. They tend their gardens and their children, who live just down the block. They believe in church and the PTA. Their homes begin to hum at sunrise and the workday begins.

Other people begin to itch after a week or month in the same locale. They check out the horizon, the other side of the mountain. They're always moving, if only in their heads. Holding the wheel, feeling the animal purr under the hood, the turning wheels like music of the spheres. The endless reverie, as if the motion of auto or plane creates an extended emptiness for dreaming.

Earth people. Nomads. Farmers and wanderers. Down through the ages.

There is a point where every trip takes on a life of its own, where the beginning is buried beyond the reach of the rearview mirror and the destination seems to slip from consciousness and there is nothing, nothing at all but the road and its pull, and that is where the road becomes irresistible and I become the road.

—Charles Bowden

Winter on the Mediterranean

(TWO NATURAL SKETCHES)

I

At a café along the beach
two Englishmen stripped to the waist
    barely moving,
like a rare species of brown toad.

Bored with travel, their bulbous bellies
are offered up without a word
    to the sun
an old, bronze coin from the sea.

2

The French woman (a Swede or Dane)
    stands ankle deep in the surf
        swaying to a winter song.

She is an aging crane, uncertain of her
    sea legs, slightly plump
        bothered by her bikini.

The whole scene is slightly out of balance—
    the camera had too much wine,
        or the winds blew in from Africa.

Women in a Spanish Fishing Village

Arm in arm women hold their daughters close
    on the way to the market. Heavy bodies homely
        in gray knee socks and flowered slippers.

I wonder what they whisper to these girls,
    what mysteries passed on about the sea, the dark
        spirits, the cruel pull of the moon.

Some women rival the padre in black sweaters
    and shawls, becoming fat, letting themselves go
        for another life without seduction or sex.

The beauty of a raven comes with old age
    when chin and nose are a knife on the crone's face,
        a sly smile when a boy-child spills his bike or blood.

For men wasting in bodegas there are sounds like gravel,
    toothless words, gestures pointing to orange peels
        and empty bottles slushing against the shore.

Spanish Photograph

The bulldozer left yesterday
    leaving a pile of rocks, several boulders
        waist high.

Today a man pounds them with a sledgehammer
    his body jolted with each blow
        like stiff dough folding onto itself.

How many years can Francisco do this
    before he is reduced to pieces
        small enough for the new condominium?

Sex in Scotland

We had come too far north of England to really enjoy the body.
    The Johns had preceded us—Calvin and Knox.

Flesh is rather scarce on the sidewalks of Aberdeen, in buses
    or pastry shops, behind bookshelves—no miniskirts here.

The incarnate Scotland hides behind closed doors—their fondness
    for beige and gray, practical fibers, simple styles.

Sex is doubtless against the law—a dark thing creeping under
    the pews of empty churches, like the stains left by seagulls.

The youth save their juice for dreaming of a sunbaked beach
    in the south—Oh, to wake up naked in someone's arms.

Gino's in Stonehaven

Let me spell it: G-I-N-O-S. That's Stonehaven, twenty minutes
    southeast of Aberdeen. An Italian restaurant in Scotland.

We knew it was special when the soups arrived: potato in a light
    beef broth, minestrone with fresh vegetables.

With the entrees, a golden light from Tuscany flooded our table.
    Lasagna—the aura of garlic gracing the tongue—piping hot.

Mona had tortellini with bits of ham in a rich cream sauce.
    The zing of scallions and red pepper.

I wanted to break into song like a gondolier on a Venetian canal.
    Each bite an aria. Tomato sauce with oregano, thyme, onion.

The desserts bordered on the indecent—Italian pudding dusted
    with cocoa, nutmeg and cinnamon, a three-flavored gelato.

I paid the bill and headed for the kitchen. Gino met me, thinking
    I had complaints: "The garlic?" he asked, "Is all right?"

"Perfection!" I said kissing my fingertips. "The best meal we've
    had in Britain." The other patrons smiled and politely clapped.

I think Gino wanted to hug me, if such were common in Scotland.
    "Ciao Gino! Grazie, molto grazie!"

Reverie in Sweden

So late in the season, the campsite was officially closed,
    but we stayed anyway.
The mist hung like a gray net over the sea.

On the toilet I think of all the Swedish fannies that sat
    here before. In fact, fannies of all nations—
a United Nations experience.

And how many will sit here next season, and the next,
    a friendship with the human family over the years.
Walt Whitman would have understood this moment.

The Almond in Winter

1

The end of a season,
our spirits lean towards the bloodless almond,
a gatherings of withered peasants rooted to the hillside.

We watch the squall shake the black spider branches,
brittle trunks. Only something shriveled by the hot sun
could wear such a face for winter.

Drafts chill our ankles, the propane is lit.
Children's eyes fill with questions. Darkness, solstice.
The time for tales.

2

Late in January the almond blooms, pink and white petals
cover the spindly arms. In the heart of winter,
a spring breeze none of us could feel.

The brown buds were a harbinger of Spring,
natives pointed them out, but the flowers are too early
to be convincing.

My stomach rolls from the sweet smell, its excess.
Too much clings from the old year, fruit from the harvest,
vials of oil enough for Easter cake and pudding.

Winter is not through with us, how foolish to pretend
otherwise. And yet life begins that way—rebirth in the bones
of ancient trees.

Ancient Deities

Shepherds first brought the tales and wild dreams down from the hills. Into the small towns where a sacred tree or bubbling spring was worshiped side by side with the Olympians.

Small chapels perched on lonely peaks where wind and thunder still speak a primitive tongue. Bunches of flowers drying over the doors, ribbons and amulets clipped to the backs of children's coats, out of reach.

In the middle of Athens, main avenues bend around small, ancient churches. Just inside the door of the sanctuary is the ever-present barrel of olive oil, the *primus materia*. The rancid smell of the last pressing floats along the streets.

Roads twist and turn in absurd patterns to navigate the groves of olive trees, which seem to be of such antiquity they stretch back to the beginning—even before the arrival of Athena.

Innocence

Parked in downtown Athens at Easter time. Maia—two years old—stands in the driver's seat of the VW bus and pretends to drive.

She is the goddess of spring—in training—turning the steering wheel back and forth, imitating her father.

From a nearby bench an old Greek with white hair and wrinkles watches Maia, how she follows her fantasy through the cosmos.

He gets up, goes in a store, buys a candy bar and brings it back to her. This aging Hermes waits briefly for a toothy smile from the Nordic cherub, pats her head and walks away.

I carry Maia on my back through the crowded streets. People passing by seem glad to see her. In the shops, she is given small gifts. I am puzzled by the ritual.

Finally, I ask a store owner, "What is it about Greeks and children?"

"Innocence," the owner replies. "Innocence comes once in a lifetime, and then it is gone. Children remind us of the innocence we once had and lost forever."

When we visit the father of Kostas high in the mountains of Crete, this lovely man with moustache and salt-and-pepper hair lifts Maia above his head as if he had found a prize. He is offering her to the gods and goddesses of the clouds floating white like feather pillows over the vineyard.

Eros

In an ancient creation story from Greece, Eros comes into existence after Chaos and Earth. He plays a central role in society as the "fairest among the deathless gods, who unnerves the limbs and overcomes the mind and wise counsels of all gods and all men. . . ."

Long before Freud, the Greeks understood the power of desire in human relationships and the workings of the cosmos. To this day Greece is the land of lovers, the young at heart. Every summer millions of visitors travel through the Greek Isles eager to remove the psychological trappings restricting their lives.

The Greek Legacy

On the beach at Paleochora—the south side of Crete—is a sign in English:
Nudism and camping / It is not allowed.
*The words are bent and rusty, difficult to read. Ten feet away are tents of
young bodies undressing, a beach of topless, sunburned bikinis and thighs.*

Shame on you Greeks! Your ancestors created the body, carved
   its sacred curves in marble. Once you celebrated the naked form.

For a brief time the ancient Greeks were more fully human, more
   confident and brilliant than anyone else on the Mediterranean

Than all those who followed the path of penance with thorns in their
   backs and ashes in their hair, fearful of their own image.

The Greeks measured the size of god's shoes and walked in them,
   looked in the mirror and gave deities penises and breasts.

The Greeks shed their clothes, oiled their skin, wrestled nude.
   No shame, no fig leafs, just men and women proud in their flesh.

No black robes and incense, no angry Father-Sky with holy writ,
   pointing his finger at sin, withering testicle and clitoris with his eye.

Just Zeus with his superb body, trim beard and intact foreskin,
   ready to hurl his thunderbolt, looking like the perfect warrior.

What happened to this vision? Did early Christians lose their nerve?
   Shunning sex and pagan orgy? Was it St. Anthony or Augustine?

All those saints covered their genitals with blue paint, fought flames
of eroticism in their caves, the nocturnal fantasies

Severed the bond between god and human. The spark of divinity
lost under a cloak of shame and incapacity.

O Greeks, break free again, come home to your heritage!

Arkadi Monastery

In November of 1866, under siege from a Turkish army, hundreds of men, women, and children hid in the refectory and in the munitions room of Arkadi Monastery. When Constantine Giambukákis fired into a powder keg, the explosion blew the roof off, killing the occupants and hundreds of the enemy. The martyred Cretans became a symbol for the Greek cause of independence.

The christening was held at Arkadi Monastery, seventeen miles into the mountains of Crete. An hour of winding roads, small villages, groves of ancient olive trees, a curve around a steep ravine and then the monastery, set on a high plateau, surrounded by elegant cypress trees. In the distance was Mt. Ida, the birthplace of Zeus.

When Kostas was brought here as a child, he was taken first to the refectory and shown the faded patches of dried blood in the mortar of the fountain. From a trapdoor in the ossuary, he could see where the Turkish sabers slashed the skulls of adults and children.

The abbot performed the baptism. His deeply tanned face, as used to hard labor in the fields as to sacred ritual. As a final act, he lifted the child in new, white clothes and made the sign of the cross with him—a moving symbol.

In Greek fashion, the child's father insisted that we—strangers—stay for the banquet in the nearby restaurant. People crowded together to make room for us. Pitchers of golden retsina appeared with quantities of chicken, pork, rice, fried potatoes, the ever-present cucumbers and tomatoes, *tiropita* (cheese pie) with mint, ice cream, and large oranges—the gift for travelers.

Since we were late, an old man at our table provided us with silverware. With a great flourish, he washed knives and forks using a glass of water and the tails of his white shirt.

Then the music began. The folk songs of the island, the history of occupation and freedom, the good life in the countryside. And everyone danced, from grandparents to toddlers—including the curious Nordic visitor from America. My daughters, ages six and two, got up, and wandered as if in a trance towards the musicians at the end of the room. When they were four feet away, friend Michael quietly came from behind with two chairs. There they sat like honored guests until fatigue overcame them.

Just at dawn we climbed through fields of wild thyme and clover to a small chapel overlooking the Mediterranean. In the distance was the wine-dark sea with its secret deeps, the mother of all life. Behind us were magnificent mountain peaks, protectors of ancient sanctuaries.

If the old gods—and the new ones—could be heard anywhere it was on this very spot. Out of all the darkness of war and oppression visited on this island, the people had created a beacon of light, a place where the vagaries and aspirations of history and spirit were woven of the same cloth.

Leaving Crete

The last night we told the owners of our favorite restaurant in Rethymnon that we were leaving the next day, and they brought each of us a gift—an orange for the trip. Should something happen, Charon will expect to find a coin in the mouth of the dead person, but he will accept an orange as payment for transportation across the Styx.

The ever-present old man by the door said that he knew a professor from Chicago. He did not remember his name, perhaps we might know him.

Topless on Santorini

I am not used to it, the sight of bare breasts on a beach.
    I try not to stare while I stare. I wonder if I am obvious.

On Samos, three generations of Swedes unveiled—from baby
    to grandmother—an exposure of politics as well as freedom.

Every summer, amazons from the north head south to the sea,
    eager to cast off shame and look lust in the eye.

Up and down the coastline, breasts pointed at the buttery sky,
    mounds, tepees, small hillocks, loaves of bread—

Pumpernickel, rye, French baguettes, whole wheat, sesame—
    baking and basking in the sun.

We're all pagans here, worshiping the old gods and goddesses—
    sun and rain, moon and mountain, sea and desert.

Our bodies were meant to touch other bodies. The reason for nerve
    endings, fingertips, the delicate surface of our tongues.

The world is brighter, more colors from the rainbow, when sparks
    leap from my lover's eyes like the Fourth of July.

The Gift of Language

Greeks talk vociferously, loudly, energetically. As beings of language, they love to argue, not as prelude to fighting, but for the sport of it. All those orations in Homer, the dialogues in Sophocles and Aeschylus.

Greeks talk with their heads and hands, talk in cafés and alleys, along the waterfront and on boats. As if reality can be vocalized into shape, domesticated and managed. For Socrates, speech was total recreation.

The bus driver stopped the bus, stood up and lectured some woman who wanted to stand rather than sit down on his bus. The woman caught without a ticket on the subway, lectured the conductor on his manners.

Another driver argued with a student. They both exited the bus, stood on the sidewalk, waved their hands and pointed their fingers. Finally, the student offered the driver a cigarette. They smoked, felt better and parted.

A mother and daughter hollered at each other down the block. They were carried home by a jet stream propelled by words.

On the Apollo Coast, an old man looking like Ichabod Crane stood up, shook his fist, and shouted at a passerby. He was nude except for his Greek sailor hat. Others joined in until a half dozen were shouting at each other. After a few minutes, a blessed quiet descended on the scene.

Lourdes of the Aegean

(FOR MONA)

Sunday night on the ferry Naias II, we push away from Piraeus
    and move from island to island like Odysseus.

The water looks like ink drawn from the night sky.
    Tiny churches cling like mountain goats to the hillsides.

Siros is partitioned by rock walls, reminding me of New England.
    Large swatches of color as if painted by a giant.

Swirls of tan and furze mark a crease where the island reclines
    like the thighs of a woman, and then folds into the sea.

I miss Mona. This, the first time I have visited Greece without her.
    I would take her hand, point to the blue doors and the whitewash.

We would discuss sailboats and the steady winds, Aeolus who
    blows travelers out of their routines.

I'm going to the island of Tinos, Lourdes of the Aegean, home
    of a miraculous icon draped in gold and silver.

She resides in a cream and white church, sitting like a confection
    on a high hill—the Panagia Evangelistria.

Pilgrims crawl block after block up to Our Lady of Good Tidings
    on a narrow strip of carpet fastened to the street.

I also have come to petition Mother Mary for healing—the oldest religion.
    I light a wax taper, four-feet long, and pray for Mona's cancer.

I collect a vial of water from a sanctified underground stream
    for anointing Mona's remaining breast when she arrives next week.

Drum Majors in Istanbul

They look like young drum majors, these pubescent boys—
    dressed in fancy outfits, walking or riding on a horse,
        followed by a joyous family.

White pants and shirt, black ties, vests, brilliant blue capes,
    hats with white feathers, silver sequined birds,
        trimmed in fur.

We wondered if they were royalty, little generals or sultans.
    Then the realization—the street led to the mosque
        and circumcision.

Hagia Sophia

We first saw her after leaving Barut's Guesthouse in early evening, walking up a steep, rock-walled street towards a restaurant. We turned a corner and there she was—the Church of Holy Wisdom, bathed in spotlights. At that moment, a flock of white pigeons ascended through the beams, as if they had just been released for our amazement.

Set on a hill, overlooking the city of Istanbul, she is grander than any image one might have gathered from books. Domes on domes, breasts and breasts, heaped up in magnificence. Pictures cannot do her justice.

One must stand within her vast interior and be dwarfed by space, wonder at the bowl-like ceiling that supports the central golden shell, indeed the dome of heaven itself.

First Christian, then Muslim, now a museum. For almost fifteen-hundred years, tarnished, wounded, desecrated, pillaged. She remains, overcoming history.

One evening Maia and I went to the nearest tall building to view her from above. We took the elevator to a restaurant on top and asked if we might photograph the great structure from this angle.

Hagia Sophia hovers over the area like a huge egg, the color of clay pottery, rose fading into tan. If the Greek Parthenon cultivates transcendence, a vision pointing towards the sky, then Sophia is a creature of the earth—round, nurturing, enclosing—the female cosmos.

V ▣ Mexico Magic

Travel in Mexico demands complete attention: the minor inconveniences, crowded roads, potholes, buses, and trucks. The glut of bicycles and burros, vendors and pedestrians in el centro. The prospect also of danger, the feeling that chaos lingers just on the other side of buildings falling into ruins in the middle of a field. Law and order is more tenuous in Mexico, feelings are more explosive.

With each crossing the tempo changes, the familiar falls away. New rituals emerge, a new reality. The well-worn masks of identity and status slowly dissolve. But this is not felt on the first trip, nor perhaps on the fifth. For some travelers Mexico will always be the sand beaches of Cancún and the tourist shops of Puerto Vallarta.

For me Mexico is a form of meditation. Fully present, I allow myself to be there. Clearly recorded. In two or three days we completely leave the States. There is no time to worry about all the tasks that were left behind. No fretting or regrets, no preoccupations. No time for self-doubt or recriminations of any kind.

Instead, a quiet thankfulness. A yielding to an inviolate presence, like a soft blanket of warm air washing over my eyes, filling my ears. Just so.

▣

Crossing Borders

I

*At the end of a long journey from the high plateau of Aztlán, the
Aztecs arrived on the shores of Lake Texcoco, saw an eagle perched on
a cactus with a serpent in its beak, and knew it was the promised land.
Quickly they founded an empire with pyramids, slaves and skull-racks.*

> Libertad, the huge people's market in Guadalajara, corner of Juárez
> and Independencia.
> With the Spanish for liberty and independence I hear the accents
> of Father Hidalgo and *El Grito de Dolores*.

> On the sidewalk, a man with a magic box like a tall, Turkish hat—
> he deals in dreams.
> Pay him, he rubs a blank piece of paper, sticks it in a glass door.
> In a moment he gives you a printout of your own private fantasy.
> A miracle machine. *Qué milagro!*

*Across the street the orphanage with Orozco's murals, flames of revolution on
vaulted ceilings. Campesinos breaking their chains, flexing in freedom from
Spain, rising on the backs of the* gachupines.

> On a crowded walkway over the avenue a man sits, his pants rolled up
> to the knees.
> Large sores cover his legs, like flowers with orange and red petals.
> Mexicans talk to him, shake loose some change. Tourists turn their heads,
> detour around him.

*North of the border we cultivate our afflictions behind closed doors.
We prefer our sick and elderly out of sight. Albuquerque has more
psychologists and psychiatrists than ministers and priests.*

2

*Take a look at a map—Canada is on our shoulders, we are on the back
of Mexico, which is ankle deep in oil. Juan Valdez fills Mr. Coffee with
morning brew, United Fruit changed its name to United Brands but
kept the same address.*

Americanos shop around, looking for a bargain.
    "How much is this in real money?"
    "You're so cheap I'll buy your whole family."
A crafty old-timer in a Winnebago RV shows me his money belt,
    securely stuffed with pesos.
This gringo crossed the border and was suddenly wealthy.

*Luis was a college student in the States. His family's ranch in Chiapas
paid a peon to serve his time in the army. Luis told me that Mexicans
have a different kind of back—it bends easily. Stoop labor in California
is natural.*

Should we feel guilty for fresh fruits and vegetables all winter long,
    for fields sprayed with toxins, the migrant misery?
Travel posters are covered with white sand beaches, margaritas served
    by Latin lovers.
Pedro's big sombrero is pulled down over his nap, the burro poses
    for photographs.

*To keep their shoes dry, illegals ride the backs of "coyotes" across the Rio
Grande to service the middle class in El Paso. Arabs sweep the streets in
Paris, Africans and Kurds unplug the sewers in Geneva and Berlin.*

3

Here in the Libertad, I seem to see both sides at once, as if the whole market slowly turns around time like a carrousel. Nothing is wrapped in plastic or boxed in cardboard.

One stall, then another, the tang of mango and papaya, *cabrito* roasting in green chile.

An old face like soft leather sells me a butcher knife, handmade, about fifty cents.

I prize another handmade knife from my grandfather, a kind of wetback who settled the sandy soil of northern Minnesota—it looked like Norway. Proud and poor his whole life.

Outside the market, a man with a python around his neck sells coyote grease and bottles of lizard oil. Both are guaranteed, naturally.

I buy some. We clasp hands, as if the joke is on the mayor or president.

Where is the border, you ask? I have been crossing it, again and again, ever since I left home.

Mexican Pharmacy

We'd been careful with food and water—
    even peeling the apples.
        It was futile.

Women in the market gave baby Sarah whatever
    brightened her blue eyes—
        pieces of pineapple, strawberries.

And at last a bellyache. Two trips to the farmacia
    for aspirin that tasted right—orange flavored
        rather than lime.

In front of me a peasant girl pleaded with the druggist,
    as if words could dissolve the demons
        consuming her infant.

What kind of bottled miracle did he have for this wasted
    body, all angular—a newborn
        sparrow nuzzling mother's breast.

Sadly, he shook his head and a shadow settled
    around us—it was too late for pills
        and potions.

Turning to leave she gently took her son's
    bony arms and wrapped them like
        toothpicks in her rebozo.

Salt Water

A trip into Mexico turned my middle life around.
 I slowly slipped back into my flesh
  and became my body again.

It began while snorkeling in San Carlos Bay,
 pursuing the shy parrotfish, the pudgy puffer.
  I felt my legs push against the flippers.

Then the mask, flush against my face,
 till it was creased, a red ring and the sting
  of salt on my lips.

Surveying mangos at the market, I squeezed
 into arms and fingers, oozed into the fleshy
  folds of my belly.

And I took on color. Not like a TV tan
 but as if the whole scene changed from sickly
  paste into luminous pieces of coral.

Wearing shorts and sleeveless shirts I saw
 more of myself in public. Some nights I raced
  through the dark in my skin.

Almost back then, no longer beside myself
 but within. I built sand castles with children
  so carefree they never left their bodies.

Late in the evening, young and old returned
    to the huge tub of an ocean. Just to bathe
        together, without games or strain.

To let go of all the strings, to float and sway
    like the fronds of large sea plants. The wash
        of salt water, inside and out.

North and South

Drinking shots of tequila, Luis and I watched the purple light of Sonora Bay gently roll towards the horizon. Luis was a motorcycle racer from Guanajuato and had traveled throughout Mexico.

"People in the north of my country," he said, "are not as friendly as people down south."

"This is true in the U.S.," I said. I grew up in Wisconsin and knew something about the frost coating the mouth of my Nordic ancestors, the blue, crystal sky floating in their minds.

In Europe, Germans are more uptight than Italians, but then compare Milan to any village in Sicily. Spaniards north of Madrid seem friendlier than the French living in the south of France, but are less convivial than the Andalusians on the Costa del Sol.

So how far does this go? What about Canada? Is there a point where a country is all north? Is there a village in the Arctic Circle where people are so frigid they rarely speak to each other?

Is Costa Rica or Panama all south? Are directions reversed south of the equator? Northern Australians are more laid-back than Aussies in Sydney or Melbourne.

Is there a place in the south where men and women are caught up in a perpetual, orgiastic embrace, a steady flame? Maybe the south simply slides into the tropics, an extended torpor, as if someone set a bowl of ripe melons in your lap, stuck a cinnamon stick in your mouth, removed your sandals and soaked your feet in warm coconut oil.

Markets

I avoid anonymous shopping malls in the States, where I become enervated and overwhelmed with promotions and prices, but Mexican markets—even the poorest ones—are filled with laughter and gossip, a carnival of possibility.

In Pátzcuaro the stands were close together, with narrow aisles. Young Tarascan mothers sitting on the ground, selling piles of vegetables or fruits, while nursing their babies. Bodies jostled against bodies, smells of armpits mixed with banana, orange, and mint.

To simply reach out and touch the flesh of the world. Mexico in living color. Nose, tongue, and ear are reborn in Mexico. Mine took on a life of their own, walking ahead of me probing this pile of *piñas,* sacks of seeds and herbs.

One whole corner of the Veracruz market was cluttered with gunnysacks of saffron and cinnamon bark, peppermint, rose petals, and sassafras. String bags of basil, chamomile, dill and lavender. Great spirals of garlic, square tins of anise and fennel.

In the meat section, a pig's head, trimmed and pink, stared out from the pork counter. All parts were for sale: tongue, tripe, intestines, heart, ears, feet. A burly man, his white apron covered with blood, unloaded the carcasses, laughed and talked with butchers and customers. He rode a special sling on the back of the meat truck.

Outside Guayabitos, between Puerto Vallarta and Mazatlán, a run-down stand sold pineapples and mangos. In the tropical heat, the fruit ripens quickly. The brownish rejects were heaped on a mound nearby. Like a thick cloud, the smell of rotten fruit hung in the air.

What was it like? Absolutely divine! A perfect sweet and sour, just on the verge of vinegar. Mona and I sat down immediately to eat our snack—we smiled and touched each other's hands.

Old and New

The central highlands are paved with the past,
    pre-Columbian temples, adobes melting in the sun.
    Buildings show their ribs.

The price paid by Indians in the silver mines and sweatshops,
    engraved in the cornerstone of cathedrals, the gilded
    domes of basilicas.

At the same time, a rawness, something unformed and
    primitive. Bouncing in the beds of pickup trucks,
    standing jaunty in doorways.

A raucous laughter that faces both death and despair.
    Working the oil and gas rigs, black with grime—
    songs of *borrachera.*

Mexico wears its sores on the outside of its clothes,
    as if all that is dark and painful could be worn
    like a necklace or vest.

Behind wedding bells and factory whistles is a lament
    for mestizos, caught between history and the empty
    promises of politicians.

Second-Class Bus

The bus to Pátzcuaro was filled with Tarascan Indians,
    laps crowded with nursing babies, bundles for market day.

We made regular stops to fill up the belching radiator.
    I crouched with chickens in the aisle trying to see ahead.

A large screwdriver was jammed into the ignition, the steering
    wheel dangled from a chain attached to the ceiling.

I was glad for the various saints on the dashboard, red and blue
    pom-poms hung from the mirror.

Our Lady of Guadalupe watched from the visor as we shook
    and swayed into town.

Isla de Janitzio

Launches leave regularly for the small island of Janitzio, in the middle of Lake Pátzcuaro. The front seats of our boat were wet from a recent rain shower, passengers huddled together. Then the weather cleared and the landing was dead ahead.

We made this pilgrimage to pay homage to José María Morelos, Creole clergyman, guerilla leader, visionary, friend of indigenous peoples. He fought for independence from Spain, was caught and executed by royalists in 1815.

A path winds upwards from the dock to his statue, forty meters high, on a large knoll. Past food stands, which form the front room of Tarascan lean-tos clinging to the hillside.

I felt uncomfortable looking directly into their homes, their beds and personal belongings. Women and children fried the famous white fish coated with egg batter. The air was heavy with blackened grease. In wooden carvings, Tarascan fishermen throw out their exquisite butterfly nets from small boats on the lake. A fishing ballet as the wings made of cord float out over the water.

Morelos holds the torch of justice; an inner, spiral staircase is lined with murals of his life. A death mask rests in the statue's head.

Returning to the launch, we found the same group we arrived with, but now the spirit was awakened. Mexicans seize any excuse for celebration. We had survived the climb, the food and the blessing. We were no longer strangers, it was time for a fiesta on the return trip. People sang and clapped—sad songs about broken hearts, joyous songs about love and adventure.

As we approached the mainland, I turned to the Mexican next to me and told him he had a wonderful voice—such passion and gusto, like Vicente Hernandez. He promptly stood up, introduced himself, and then his wife, son, and daughter. Then it was my turn with my family. *Mucho gusto* all around. We told them we loved Mexico, their faces lit up like fireflies in the night.

Roberto Estrade was an immigration officer from Ciudad Juarez. And we were from Albuquerque, New Mexico, not far away. Come and visit. Yes, you are always welcome. We met again in the parking lot with handshakes all around and *buen viaje*.

They drove away in a large Dodge station wagon with Ohio license plates and I remembered tales about cars disappearing south of the border. We climbed into our VW bus and headed for the campgrounds.

Spring Break in Mazatlán

By the central market downtown,
    a mother slips out of the crowd waiting for a bus,
walks her two-year-old to the curb
    unzips his pants and points his penis into the street.
A small stream of urine splashes the cobblestones,
    as if he were a fireman.
They get back in line.

On the beach in front of the Costa del Oro
    frat boys from Texas Tech in matching tank tops
    carry cans of Tecate like toting jars of testosterone.
One of them detours to a stone wall, gropes in his shorts
    points his penis, and an arc of urine hits the rocks,
    as if he were a fireman.
He returns to his friends and a high five all around.

Paradise

A North American opens the gate to the El Dorado Trailer Park and says, "Welcome to paradise!" He is right. After hundreds of miles on narrow roads without shoulders, after sucking up the fumes of a Pemex gas truck on Tepic hill, we have arrived safely in heaven—we might stay indefinitely.

How can you be a failure at a Mexican beach?
Leaving old measures of success behind us,
we've come all this way with tent, lawn chairs,
ice chest, aloe vera, extra batteries and kids.

We bathe in the purple light of evening,
gently bobbing like corks in the sensuous swells.
Our claims to prestige vanish in the warm salt water.
We are once more our bodies floating in the womb.

We talk—where are you from? Where are you going?
Manzanillo? San Blas? Yucatán or Belize?
What about chiggers, margaritas in a fishbowl?
Does your van ping on the gas, the perfect beach?

Road warriors have a common lexicon of suffering
and endurance. We don't care about answers, having
driven beyond truth or memory. It is simply the caress
of the human voice, birds flying around in our heads.

Roadkill

Leaving the Chapala RV Park south of Guadalajara, I drove into the small village of Ajijic and a supermarket. By the side of the road was a dead tan and white colt, stiff as a piece of marble. Like a statue, a second horse stood with its head extended over the colt, staring downwards. A guardian perhaps, waiting for the spirit to gently rise out of the bruised flesh.

Across the narrow road also on her side, the mare with the same tan and white markings, bloated with four stiff legs sticking straight out.

The two horses had been killed during the night, probably by a truck or bus. Most trucks are equipped with a heavy, steel framework on the front fenders and grill. On long, boring stretches of highway, some truckers play chicken with animals that drift through fences to feed near the road.

I tried to imagine what happened, but wonder how a large, powerful machine passing through the village could possibly kill both horses, leaving them on opposite sides of the road. In the stillness of early morning, the mare and her colt were probably grazing on the sweet grasses near the pavement. With the roar of the diesel, they looked up, switching their tails. At home with each other, even in the glare of headlights.

The driver had to smack their torsos with enough force to kill and divide them without dragging their bodies unto the hood of the truck and a possible accident. He was either very skilled or the truck was so big it easily left death in its wake.

What then shall we call the carnal remains of these horses? Neither *corpse* nor *cadaver* seem appropriate. *Carcass* is usually reserved for animals slaughtered for meat, not slaughtered for the pleasure of a male ego.

Dead bodies are common along Mexican highways, especially dogs. Usually I slough their images like I speed past roadkill in the States. From childhood came memories of cows covered with flies, waiting for the rendering truck. We even told each other jokes about the glue factory.

But these bodies were not located in a pasture, a niche in the natural order of things, but along a village street. Stock-still, the three of them made a statement and demanded some kind of response.

Clutching the steering wheel of my van, I began to sob. Great swells of sadness erupted out of some reservoir within. All the pieces of suffering neatly tucked away since entering Mexico—street kids sorting through garbage, withered women touching my arm for a handout, young indigenous mothers with toddlers selling Chiclets. Men with twisted limbs scooting along on little platforms with wheels.

The previous day in Pátzcuaro, I had stopped by the roadside to watch a colt try out his legs as if they were a new set of springs. Bouncing one way, then another. Next he raced full bore across the field. With a fanfare of tossing mane and tail, the young horse pranced before his mother. The very picture of animal energy and innocence, the painful, almost unbearable joy of *la primavera*— the prime of life. I called him Pegasus.

Maps

(FOR MONA)

In love with maps, ordinary road maps, with tiny tables
    for rest areas, red teepees for campgrounds.

I search for a white van along a Mexican highway and find
    a crushed rose hidden in the fold,

as beautiful dried as when I bought it fresh in Veracruz
    for five pesos, a surprise for Mona.

The whole end of the market was filled with flowers.
    I felt lightheaded, almost foolish in the scented air.

"*Para mi esposa*," I told the *florista*, who then added
    greens and fussed until finished.

There are no shortcuts around such transactions
    in a country that cherishes ceremony.

This was not the Midwest with its cool efficiency,
    but a Latin celebration.

With a flourish he bowed and gave me a work of art.
    "*Mil gracias*," I said, this delightful diversion.

That night on the plaza, shrimp in a red lace of garlic
    marimbas played in front of the restaurant.

Not just memories, but maps. Two lives at a crossroads,
    we continue to intersect, our journey together.

Mazatlán Airport

(FOR PAT AND RUDY ANAYA)

Waiting for Pat and Rudy at the slightly worn airport
    in a sling chair at the observation window. In the sky
    is a silver cigar sailing through the heavens.
    No, even smaller—the size of a cigarette or popsicle stick.

Is it possible that Pat and Rudy are sitting in that shiny missile,
    strapped in, prepared to land beyond the east concourse?
    What size are they, since they fit inside that glistening tube?
    The windows are a line of dots, the wings are two feathers.

When will they take on normal size to show their passports
    at immigration? Then walk the corridor, down the stairs,
    pick up their luggage, push the button for a green or red light
    at the checkpoint and feel the excitement of arrival.

They will exit the double doors into the lobby, smell the salt
    from the Sea of Cortés, the soft, tropical air on their faces.
    I will welcome them in my arms and breathe a sigh of relief—
    they have arrived at one of the beautiful beaches of the world.

Timing is Everything

Sarah's high school graduation trip to Mazatlán began with a hot train ride through the Sonoran desert. The air conditioning was broken, so she cooled herself on the open platform at the rear of the train.

Finishing a Coke, she caught herself before heaving the can into cactus and mesquite. "Ecology," she said, and carried the empty container inside the stifling compartment. Jostled by crates of chickens and nursing mothers, she threw it into a receptacle.

Just then a porter came down the aisle collecting all the trash in a large garbage bag. He carried the bulging sack to the platform at the end of the train and ceremoniously unloaded it beside the tracks, which twisted like a lazy snake behind them.

The Dust of Mexico

There is saying that once the dust of Mexico has settled on your heart
there can be no rest for you in any other land.

In the autumn, when the geese honk overhead going south, I spread
      my feathers and follow the sun.
Just to slip over the border, like sloughing off my clothes.

No matter how many times I've made this crossing, it is ever
      the first time. A smile creeps into my feet, they begin to tap.
The seams leak and starch runs out of my shirt.

Northwest of Guaymas is San Carlos, where the Sonoran desert unrolls
      like a carpet to the edge of the sea. Jagged, razor-back mountains.
The clear skeleton of mesa ringed by fifty miles of light.

On the dry hillsides, scrub, saguaro cactus, lizards doing push-ups.
      God-like gulls with black trim tilt along the horizon.
In the evening, blues and purples wash across the dunes and rock.

We stand on the beach with one foot in water, the other on shore—
      both dry and wet, one extreme touches the other.
Licking salt from our lips, salt water running through our veins.

Mona and I are king and queen of a patch of tents and children's
      toys, castles and towers that wash out with the waves.
There is no other place we'd rather be, nothing is missing.

We envy no one—their condos in Hawaii, chalets in the Alps.

The very best time of our lives. With our family, the circle
is complete. Always today. Today, always.

In some part of my dreams, I walk this beach every night
in the transparency of scented air,
talking with pelicans and seagulls, listening to waves hit the sand.

VI ❧ The Common Life

Finally there is only one story worth telling, one poem
that we write over and over; the same poem that all other
poets have been writing over the ages. The same myth
that has sparked light in children's eyes around campfires
and at bedtimes. It is the story of our journey on this
earth, following dreams, meeting other travelers who
have taken to the road in search of themselves. Looking
for adventure, longing to create a safe place for flowers
and family, where we treat each other like relatives.

In the end we are what we remember and what we
imagine—nothing more. We tend to remember those
moments when we were most intensely alive, whether
with pain or joy. We search for a common language
that would bind writer and reader together in a
spiritual communion.

Labyrinth

Mine is the labyrinth, not the heroics of high noon.
    A mind filled with weeds, endless rooms
        filing cabinets and books.

A life of small objects, artifacts and mementos,
    like the stone with a hole through it
        from old Epidauros.

Mediterranean sick went to the center
    of healing. The god Asclepius, dream rooms,
        oracular snakes from under the floor.

But I'm not Greek, not Anglo or Saxon.
    My ancestors didn't build the drive-in or bank.
        They farmed the rocky hillsides

With one eye on the glacier. They chewed the edges
    of their shields before battle, wooed women
        with scales from beneath the fjords.

I need an amulet for my neck—two eyes like currants,
    a magic bone, a Boy Scout compass,
        my whole family on a leather thong.

My home is the road. Nordics have always moved
    south, to mango mornings and pineapple skies.
        There's frost on the back of my head.

En Route to School in the East

Camped a night in the front seat of my car,
    some antique mining town strapped to a rocky hillside,
        the middle of Pennsylvania.

Awakened at sunrise, a face pressed to the window.
    Said I was parked illegally by the meeting house,
        asked would I like to come and eat with the family.

I said, I've left home for the first time—Wisconsin.
    And now, far from the toll road, I'm here,
        thirsty for some coffee. I was given a full cup.

Burly sons and daughters, up at sunrise for work.
    Help yourself to blue mist and pancakes, they said.
        We do battle with these mountains after breakfast.

Daughter of Eve

Sarah had gotten me so angry
    I took off my shirt
        and threw it at her.

But that night when I went
    to kiss her mischievous head—
        a ritual of four and a half years

she reached out in her sleep
    pulled me close
        and kissed my cheek.

Love catches us like that—
    hot and cold,
        turning in both directions.

How Would You Like It, Dad?

Sarah always believed a good offense is the only defense.
    Never admit you're wrong, never admit defeat.

Stand there toe-to-toe. Even with all the evidence—her room
    filled with dirty clothes, the rabbit's empty food dish.

How would you like it, dad? she yells, her feet planted solid.
    Well, how would you?

I wouldn't. But we play out our roles anyway, to the end.
    One a mirror image of the other. Her eyes wet like mine.

Mastectomy
(From the Greek mastos, *a breast,*
and -ectomy, *the removal thereof)*

I

First a lump was found in Mona's breast. A biopsy confirmed the worst.
  Perhaps a lumpectomy, but then a second shadow, another biopsy—
  two spots of cancer, almost invisible.

Time both sped up and slowed down, as if an event had to be wrested
  from the ordinary spin of daily life. Advice from books and experts,
  and then a decision.

Medical voices might say something different next year, but sharp winds
  were blowing towards Mona, like knives cutting down fields
  of wheat.

Science with its cool demeanor said a breast must be cut off, a piece of
  meat sent to the lab, then discarded. The oncologist said so, all available
  data agreed.

We thought a woman surgeon should have some feeling for breasts—
  as more than the tissue and ducts in *Gray's Anatomy*, more than lactating
  mammae.

Nurtured by them, our children first learned love with their lips and tongues.
  A nursing mother, a nursing infant—at once, both food and rapture,
  the original Garden of Eden.

For me also, breasts were beauty and bliss, the bounty of passion. Holding
  on to each other and held. But cancer had moved into her body, a
  shadow casting dice.

The breast that had given suck and solace must be sacrificed, as certain as day
  turning into night. Beloved friends gathered for ceremony and support.
  On May 14, 1999, Jean Wright cut off Mona's right breast.

2

We brought Mona home one day after surgery, Saturday noon. Daughters
   arrived to tend to their mother. I say prayers for children who hold tight
   to our lifelines, lest in age or illness we drift away.

The dressing on the wound was to be changed the next day. Sunday
   morning, Maia said, "Mom isn't ready for you to see her without
   the bandage." It would not be easy for any of us.

Named for the Goddess of Spring, Maia conceived a plan—she would
   shower with her mother, together, both naked as the morning of her
   birth on Easter Sunday years before.

I can only imagine the tears they shed together—mother and daughter—
   as they viewed the incision, a red line thick as a pencil stretching
   from breastbone to armpit, running halfway across the chest.

They showered the whole area, as if bathing in a warm rain, slightly
   concave now, unbalanced, the world out of sorts. Then daughter
   rubbed oil into the violated flesh.

Each sweep of her hands told her mother she was beautiful, her body
   was sacred, this amazing being who created life—first one, then two
   and three—Peter, Sarah, and Maia.

"Now I am ready," Mona said. "There is nothing to hide from you.
   For thirty-four years we've been wife and husband, lovers and friends.
   We're sun and moon, earth and sky, to each other."

Take, for Example, Ralph

What else could he be other than dog?!
Comes inside, rolls on his back into I-trust-you-posture.
Is uneasy exposing himself this way.
The hair circling his penis is yellow-stained.

The mailman approaches the door, Ralph barks—it works.
He barks at meter maids and dogs on leashes—it works.
Ralph deals with buzzing cicadas. He eats them—crunch.
He'll eat most anything—rotten breath.

Walking the street, Ralph checks out hydrants—suspicious.
A van pulls up, asks, "What kind is it? Mine's half-Samoyed,
half-husky. Looks just like yours." Startled, I ponder Ralph,
half-Samoyed, half-mutt, I don't think of him as *Mine*.

Neighbors rush to greet us as he veers away from the roses,
one leg in the air. A Texan in a motel parking lot defended
his oil painting from Ralph and declared,
"It might not be worth a damn, but you can't piss on it."

I like the way Ralph growls at dogs that sniff his rear
then trots to the nearest bush and gives it both legs,
even if he's empty. I'd like to do that when someone
checks out my credit or questions my self-esteem.

I once found a large school tablet in the attic filled with
childhood portraits: page after page of a stick boy
peeing on a burning bush—a young lad with his own hose
and a powerful arc into green flames. A dog's fantasy.

Ralph farts in his sleep and snores like a buzz saw.
So do I. Dreams about chasing cats up a tree. Tail wags.
Thinning out and gray in the muzzle, slower reflexes.
No regrets, no midlife crisis, no myth of Sisyphus.

If you meet the Buddha on the road, it's probably Ralph.

Neighbors Is Neighbors

For years he was a lumberjack in Oregon, wearing down his legs
on the steep coastal range. Had come with his wife to Colorado
in a truck. They were tenting across the way from us, in the Rockies.

They said, It's not very friendly between here and there. They
don't even have a Welcome to Utah sign coming into that state.
At the first service station, they didn't even ask to check my oil.
You can bet I didn't mention it, he said.

Mornings he left early to cut trees, returning with his lunchbox
full of bear claw mushrooms, which he shared. You cook them the
same way you cook steak—a little onion and hot grease.

One evening I went over to borrow some coffee—we'd said a
few words at the water pump and waved when he came from work.
They gave me a whole can of Folgers. When I protested, they said,
Neighbors is neighbors ain't they? We made enough brew for two
more, and chatted past sunset.

After a Storm on the Costa del Sol

(FOR MONA)

Yesterday a typhoon from North Africa,
    white foam, a frenzy of winds, broken boats.

Waves cut into the old banks, the beach
    was crimson.

Today the sea is a sheet of vinyl, laced with blue foil.
    The sky is empty and terribly still.

We hardly move. It is our turn, as if words could bind
    one life to another and heal the hurt.

I want to say some damage is necessary—barnacles swept
    from the rocks, the old skin rubbed away.

Tomorrow we will stand at dawn where deep swells
    wash and feed beds of purple mussels.

Rooted in perfect rows at the very edge of the water,
    great slabs of rock farmed by the sea.

Millennium Two Thousand

It has begun again like shifting plates on the ocean floor, that momentous
   turning over of time, that upheaval in the linings of the stomach—

When one age dies and another is born. Recorded in the heavens the sun
   cycle moves from the legend of Pisces to the vision of Aquarius.

Early this century, seers and magicians saw it coming—Blavatsky and
   Rudolph Steiner, Krishnamurti and Edgar Cayce—the list is long.

But this time as the serpent swallows its tail, the spiral moves up a notch
   on the eternal cycle. A new tooth is added to the gear.

Persephone's husband also eats the pomegranate and both ascend from
   Hades to meet Mother Demeter, and Orpheus does look back.

Theseus winds his way into the Cretan labyrinth to embrace the Minotaur
   and they dance together out of the cave.

This time Moses descends from Mt. Sinai and rubs palm oil on the Golden
   Calf. Crossing the Jordan, he kisses the Palestinians on both cheeks.

This time Brutus and Cassius throw Caesar a party, and Anthony brings
   Cleopatra a pet monkey rather than a snake.

Jesus shuns penance. He finds a loving wife and they have children in
   a bower of almond petals. He leaves his keys to Mary Magdalen.

This time no one chases Muhammad out of Mecca, he buries his sword
   in the desert while dreaming about paradise.

Guinevere has an identical twin sister named Guinevere for Lancelot. Authur asks the right question at Castle Perilous. Napoleon is eight inches taller.

When Humpty-Dumpty falls on his head, all the king's horses and men put him together again, and Henny-Penny is taken seriously.

This time we will join native peoples in the Ghost Dance, the buffalo returns, along with the passenger pigeon and the dodo bird.

The Melting Pot becomes a crazy quilt with black, brown, red, yellow, straights, gays, Jews, Christians, Buddhists, pagans, and Unitarians.

No religious group claims ultimate, exclusive truth, since all spiritual paths—East and West—lead to the same place.

This time, no more breast cancer, no more cancer of any kind, and people turn off their TV sets so they have time for poems and storytelling.

And my story begins like this: Every day, Mona and I repeat a miracle—we fall in love and have three bright, compassionate children.

We hitch a ride on this amazingly beautiful blue planet into the new millennium, thankful for each other and a thousand blessings.

Wondering about Things

1

Driving in a downpour, just the two of us
   Sarah's young fancy began to roam—

Dad, when you were a kid, did you wonder
   about clouds and where grass comes from
      why the sky looks like the inside of a marble?

Did you ever notice how beautiful rain is
   when it hits the pavement—
      like tiny angels leaping up?

2

This morning granddaughter Zola played again
   with the manger scene, shuffling miniature camels,
      sheep, herders and Magi around the room.

She paused to announce—"Baby Jesus once worked
   in a circus, but now he's out flying."
      She's probably right.

Letter to Maia on Her Birthday

APRIL 11, 2003

In Norway, a guardian spirit of the household, Hamingja, *cares for a
child born with a caul over her head.*

Thirty-two years ago, she arrived at dawn on Easter Sunday.
　　Maia, Goddess of Spring—mother of Hermes—master of two worlds.

Born with a caul, an extra membrane—second birth for second sight.
　　Like Cassandra and Julius Caesar. Protected by a Nordic spirit.

She reads our minds, completes sentences for us, believes in ghosts.
　　Sometimes pushes me for answers too new for words.

Not always a blessing, Maia yearns for truth to pierce the veil of Isis.
　　A touchstone for feelings swirling through the house.

I barely think of me as father—of course I am and she is daughter.
　　But father has little to do with birth. Sperm is easy,
　　　　but to carry a child within is beyond any male fantasy.

I try to imagine the first time baby moves on her own,
　　her tiny heart like a drum, feel her kick from inside with both feet
　　　　learning to swim beneath my skin.

The dark nights at the edge of the world transacting a future for her.
　　Then that moment when the cave of the body opens and all
　　　　that is valued separates and slips into the burning air.

And you gaze in wonder at the perfection of your dreams.
    Tiny, cherry-red lips sucking at your breast, the sweetness
        of nipples—and your body flows into your body.

From then on, whenever you see her, you see yourself—not as mirror,
    but as if you divided. Once you were one and now you are two.
        A tether spun from the earth's umbilicus in between.

All this men will never know. Even Zeus had to invent a story
    about the baby Dionysus gestating in his thigh.

Birth blood is so powerful that Jews and Christians outlawed
    women in the temple, twisted misogyny into monastic privilege.

Men with their empty loins must create a child out of thin air—
    Bottle-feeding, diapers, water-everywhere-baths, endless books.

Fathers make good horseback rides, tumbling mats and swing sets,
    postures like pretzels, witness to first steps and crises.

I can still feel a two-year-old hand cupped in mine as we walked
    down the rocky riverbed to the Sea, searching for treasure—

bits of plastic hose, half a ballpoint, a sardine can, a soft rubber ring,
    one green lemon from Africa, three pinecones, and five seashells.

Exhausted from scouring the beach, she climbed to my shoulders
　　for the journey home, a lunch of anchovies and cream cheese.

Maia learned to run in the Alhambra—a Moorish ghost startled her
　　two-year-old legs into a precarious hands-in-the-air, teeter-totter
　　across a marble floor. A Moroccan silversmith smiled.

All the mornings we walked to school, the myriad miles down the road,
　　the Holidays waiting at the airport for Maia's return. Joyful times,
　　　but desperation as well, when the world cracked open.

In my reveries, a radiant person walks by and I know we are related,
　　a silver thread runs from my heart to the heart of my daughter—
　　　we are forever connected wherever we are.

I see it, she sees it, and we never talk about it. One could use the word
　　"love" but it is so much closer. I'm a clay pot filled with memories.
　　　The future shines like a golden ring.

Bird Watching

Genuine bird-watchers record the names of rare birds seen in habitats around the globe in official bird-watcher notebooks. I want to publicly note that I have observed the same sixty-three pelicans on the same coastline, doing the same damn thing day after day.

If seagulls are the test pilots, the acrobatic, coastal show-offs, then pelicans are the gentlemanly B-52s, strong and steady, slightly dated in appearance, and often comic. Mornings and evenings they fly across the bay in squadrons of four to fourteen on fish patrol, dipping down close to the water, scanning the swells for schools of finny food.

With their incongruous bodies, they look like elder statesmen who have spent their lives in the hors d'oeuvres—a skin pouch under the chin, cocked head, a paunch for a stomach. Built more for confrontation, than elegant flight.

With a powerful wing thrust, one will break from the group, climb thirty or forty feet and dive for his breakfast. For a time he looks good, as if he were following some instinctual program: wings slightly bent for steering, head pointing down like a spear, feet neatly folded. But then he crashes into the water and it looks like his appendages come unhooked, his whole body flies apart.

This meeting of bird and water is a disaster, as if the bird had missed the entire second half of the diving-for-breakfast lessons. One can't imagine how pelican parents ever teach the young ones about gathering food. After a parent demonstrates colliding with water, one can hear baby bird exclaiming, "Are you crazy? I'd rather stand in the shallows with herons and scoop out little fish as they swim by."

The pelicans themselves pretend to be oblivious of their kamikaze plunges. After the explosion of spray and feathers, they quickly pull their wings together and briefly regain their dignity, sitting all tucked in, coyly floating in place.

One afternoon a big brown pelican landed within twenty feet
of our camp. It looked sickly and crouched close to the ground
with a sad, wizened expression. Had it come to die? Was it deranged
by pesticides or brain parasites? For a moment we had the New
Age fantasy that this bird was an emissary from another dimension.
The great beak of the pelican would open like a prophet and
speak in the ancient language of salt and sea:

> Listen to me you pale skins without scales or wings!
> The world is either fat or fire, wet or dry,
> You either get heavy and sink, or grow feathers and fly.

Nodding his elongated head like a preacher satisfied with his
sermon, he lumbered into the air and disappeared across the bay.

Spring Rites

I feel so prickly alive
    my hair stands straight up—
        yet it doesn't make sense.

I'm in debt & overweight
    the president's a crook,
        it's only the 1st of March.

But kids are roller-skating
    Sarah has a lemonade stand
        Mona bought seed for the garden.

I feel tiny tendrils growing between
    my toes. Without fanfare
        I hug the peach tree.

A Season without God

1

Autumn is the time for barricades, recriminations.
   Hot winds dry the leaves on the trees, shrivel them
   like pieces of skin, the parchment of old books.

Under heavy gourds and melons the salt taste of blood.
   Beneath the Eiffel Tower the small tongues of children.
   Their bones leave an imprint in the sand.

This is the season for heroes. Joan of Arc stares fondly
   at her sword. Moses climbs the mountain and returns.

2

All this must stop in winter—
   Snow on the ground, we sit like stones in a circle.

Hair stiffens like the bare branches of oak. Moments
   stretch across the lake in sheets of ice.

This is the meaning of peace—to look at each item in turn.
   The withering leaves. The bare thistle. The sullen sky.

To see with quiet eye—a lover's hand suddenly limp, white.
   Noisy crows in the treetops. Six loaves of black bread.

We are simply here—with every other thing.

Epiphany

There's not a day
　　I'm not amazed
　　　　by God's excess.

Yesterday
　　birds filled every branch
　　　　of our apple tree.

Today
　　a young friend
　　　　had her womb removed.

Emergence

(ON THE BIRTH OF DAVID JAMES—MARCH 17, 2004)

MARCH 15

Mona and I came to the City of Angels to witness the birth
    of our grandson, to wait for time itself to bear fruit.

Maia's belly was a soft bumper sticking out and beyond.
    We watched her caress it, amazed—Can this really be me?

Mother and father spoke to that stomach, told baby they
    loved him. Maia listened to her body, learning to let go.

That evening I took my chair to the beach for a talk with Ocean,
    salt-mother of all life. The waves were regular and strong.

Fog and mist out to the horizon. This event is outside my wishes
    or schedule. We're not on clock time now,

but the rhythm of generations, the cycle of the life force.
    Maternity wards are busiest when there's a full moon.

Maia had a dream last night. David was born, she saw his face,
    his red hair. Something larger than self was taking over.

She kissed the bottoms of his feet. His birth will be soon,
    perhaps within three days. We must be patient.

THE AFTERNOON OF MARCH 16

Walking the dogs, up the hill in the RV park when Maia called,
 her water broke at the housing bureau, downtown L.A.

She was headed for Cedars-Sinai with Mona. It was beginning.
 Pete asked me to get their camera, fate supplied a parking space.

Without the amniotic shield, infection for mother and child was
 likely. Labor could begin on its own, but didn't.

Doctor Tsui chose to induce, hoping dilation would take place.
 It might be one centimeter per hour, with a goal of ten.

Probably a long wait. We moved to a sacred place between hope
 and fear, the threshold before and after life.

With the night ahead, I returned to the trailer and the dogs.
 The Imperial Highway was bumper-to-bumper.

The beach was lit with fireworks, the Persian New Year.
 Didn't anyone realize my daughter was giving birth?

I dozed until 2 A.M., then decided to return to the hospital.
 My stomach ached. I took this as an omen.

Maia was moved to a chilly birthing room. Mona and Pete
    wore white blankets like a scene from *Lawrence of Arabia*.

Contractions came too hard and fast so Tsui stopped inducing.
    Maia rested and waited in a quiet, twilight zone.

All hoped surgery could be avoided. Nurse Susan, the angel,
    arranged for the miracle. Maia's own labor took over.

About 6 A.M., Susan felt David's head in the birth canal.
    Now Maia felt the contractions and leaned into the pain.

Grandmother and father were cheerleaders, holding Maia's legs.
    One big breath, exhale, new breath, hold and push down.

She was heroic, her time on center stage. Beyond the lightning
    in her thighs was the passage of her child.

Three more breaths and he crowned. A pause, Tsui cut the cord
    around David's neck. Two more and a baby boy was born.

With expert massage, his tiny body slipped into rhythms of pink
    and cream. So exquisite—lips and cheeks, fingers and toes.

No stork for this wonder child, but emergence—from the depths
    of his water-world, into the open arms of family.

MIRACLE ON MARCH 17, 7:21 A.M.

Not miracle as overturning science or reason, raising the dead
or changing water into wine.

But the miracle of awaking from a dream. Birth is as everyday
as Canadian geese flying in a flawless vee.

Not super-natural, but nature itself. The life force steals your
breath, like the shimmer of gold in a field of sunflowers.

Birthing a child is different from staring at stars in the night sky.
You turn the telescope around, look deep rather than vast.

The eye turned on the mystery within. The elemental rhythm,
like feeling the drumbeat inside your bones.

The crowning of David James took us to the threshold of spirit—
flesh of our flesh, creator and creation.

As Maia birthed her son, a chorus of ancestors cheered her on—
parents, grandparents, uncles and aunts.

Encircled by prayer, an eternal flame lit the core of his being.
Anointed with his natal waters, each breath a benediction.

Every child is the chosen one, every newborn the messiah.
This is the gift—time renewed, darkness transformed into light.